HISTORICAL RECORDS AND STUDIES

THE MONOGRAPH SERIES

THOMAS FRANCIS MEEHAN
(1854 - 1942)

MONOGRAPH SERIES: XX

THOMAS FRANCIS MEEHAN
(1854 - 1942)

A MEMOIR
by
SISTER M. NATALENA FARRELLY
Sisters of St. Joseph
Brentwood, New York

NEW YORK
THE UNITED STATES CATHOLIC
HISTORICAL SOCIETY
1944

PUBLICATION COMMITTEE
Rev. Thomas J. McMahon, S.T.D.

S. Sterns Cunningham   Richard Reid

Rev. W. Eugene Shiels, S.J., Ph.D.

OFFICE OF
THE EXECUTIVE SECRETARY OF THE SOCIETY
SUITE 103
924 WEST END AVENUE, NEW YORK 25, NEW YORK

TABLE OF CONTENTS

PREFACE

THIS Memoir of an indefatigable student of Catholic origin is offered to the members of the United States Catholic Historical Society as a tribute to one who for many years was proud to devote his richest labors to its cause. The best monument to Thomas Francis Meehan is the Society's own treasury, *Records and Studies,* which is practically a catalog of his published works. And who shall say how many other volumes invaluable to the historian owe to this friend of students, if not their actual existence, at least much of their inspiration, their accuracy, their fullness?

Only those who knew Thomas Meehan intimately can appreciate the heights and depths which lay behind his contribution to Catholic historical scholarship. His sterling practical Catholicity, his broad culture, the fine balance which he knew how to preserve between scholarly detachment and warm human sympathy,—these are qualities which his friends remember with reverence. The present work is in no sense a complete biography, but only an attempt to present in an orderly form, against the background of an exceptionally busy life, the contribution made by Thomas Meehan to the preserving and continuing the systematic record of Catholic achievement in the New World. His life was indeed a long litany of worthy accomplishments, full of services rendered without thought of personal glory. To tell the full story would require successive studies of Thomas Meehan, the writer; Thomas Meehan, the editor and compiler; Thomas Meehan, the wise and humble counsellor. The Reverend John J. Wynne, S. J., an historian himself, spoke truly when he said, "It would take a Fra Angelico to paint a true picture of Thomas F. Meehan."

The plan which has been followed in this Memoir is simple. After a preliminary study of the youthful environment, education, and early labors of Thomas Meehan, I have devoted a chapter to his association with the United States Catholic Historical Society, to which this present work is dedicated.

One of Thomas Meehan's favorite boasts was that he was "the oldest Jesuit in the Province." In Chapter Three the Reverend Francis X. Talbot, S.J., Editor of *America,* tells of the long career of distinguished service rendered to The America Press by the tireless scholar whose zeal for the cause of the Church made him an inspiration to clergy and laymen alike.

The Appendix includes a Bibliography and several excerpts from the writings of Thomas Meehan, which will serve the reader as samples of his style and spirit.

Grateful acknowledgment is owed by the writer to Mrs. Katherine Meehan Cadley, the historian's daughter, who graciously consented to the use of her father's library and answered innumerable questions about his work, and to a long list of personal friends who freely offered their recollections: Right Reverend John L. Belford, to whom go heartfelt thanks for the generous foreword, Reverend John J. Wynne, S.J., the late Reverend Paul Blakely, S.J., Dr. Blanche Mary Kelly, Cornelia Craigie, Elizabeth Herbermann, Mrs. Thomas McGoldrick, Mary Deitsch, Mrs. James Hanley, and Thomas Woodlock.

A special note of gratitude is due to Reverend Francis X. Talbot, S.J., who suggested the writing of the Memoir and contributed the chapter on *America;* and to Reverend Dr. Thomas J. McMahon, editor of the publications of the United States Catholic Historical Society, who lent constant encouragement and friendly interest. For an invaluable source of information the writer is indebted to the Right Reverend Monsignor Peter Guilday who allowed unstinted access to the personal correspondence of Thomas Meehan. Further correspondence in the Archives of the Archdiocese of New York was made accessible at Dunwoodie through the kind permission of the Most Reverend J. Francis A. McIntyre and the cooperation of Reverend Jeremiah Brennan, Archivist.

The writer is sincerely grateful to the Reverend John K. Sharp who read the manuscript and to Dr. Walter Willigan of St. John's University who gave editorial advice. She is especially happy to acknowledge her indebtedness to the Sisters of Saint Joseph of Brentwood, from Reverend Mother Jane Frances, who gave her permission to undertake the work, down to the Sister who typed the manuscript.

SISTER M. NATALENA FARRELLY, S.S.J.

FOREWORD

THIS little book is a brief account of the life and work of a great man. He was not widely known. He held no exalted office. His work made him great. He lived many years. He produced much. He rendered valuable service to truth, justice and religion. He was a thinker, a writer and a champion of the life and virtues on which Church and State rest. His light shined upon men so that they seeing his good works might give glory to the Father in Heaven Who inspired and sustained him.

He was, first of all, a gentleman. In thought, word and work, he was considerate, gentle, patient, tolerant, gracious. These are the outward signs of faith and charity. If there were a Catholic Hall of Fame, it would be incomplete without the name of Thomas Francis Meehan. His Catholicity appeared in all he did. It was the aim of his life to make it known and loved and he lost no opportunity to explain and defend it.

He was not an orator. He was a scholar and a writer. He has written much on many subjects. No man of our century has acquired and shown more knowledge of the Catholic Church and growth in this vicinity. Of that knowledge he made most generous use.

He was a disciple of the genial St. Francis. Genial himself, he saw the good and beautiful everywhere. He loved to release it and praise it with the soft voice and touching smile his heart inspired.

Eighty-eight years is long for a human life—too long for most of us. But it was not too long for him. He never lost interest in his work. He drove his pen until he could drive no more.

This book should inspire admiration and imitation. To us he says with St. Paul, "Be ye imitators of me, as I am of Christ Jesus."

RIGHT REVEREND JOHN L. BELFORD, D.D.

Feast of St. Thomas
1944.

THOMAS FRANCIS MEEHAN

Chapter I

THOMAS FRANCIS MEEHAN—HIS LIFE

1. Parentage

Culture, refinement, simplicity and a wealth of literary attainments marked the home in which Thomas Francis Meehan was born on September 19, 1854. His parents, Patrick J. Meehan and Mary Jane Butler, were both members of families prominent in Brooklyn Catholic circles. Patrick J. Meehan, who was editor continuously of the *Irish American* from 1857 to the day of his death on April 20, 1906, was born in the city of Limerick, Ireland, on July 17, 1831, of an old and respectable family, the representatives of whose branches occupied high rank in the business, agricultural and clerical walks of life in his native country.

His school days, up to his seventeenth year, were passed in one of the old time classical schools for which the "City of the Violated Treaty" was famous, and where he laid the foundation of a store of knowledge which afterwards expanded and increased by private study, made him one of the most successful journalists of his generation. His father dying while he was quite young, his mother was married a second time to the late Patrick Lynch, the founder and first editor of the *Irish American*.

After the death of O'Connell, and the gloom and disaster of '48, Patrick Lynch, like so many others who had been prominent in the political movement of that era, left Ireland and came to New York, where, after a short connection with the daily press, he established the *Irish American,* the first number appearing on

11

August 12, 1849. His family, seven in number, of which Patrick Meehan was one, then emigrated and settled in New York, moving later on to Brooklyn.

Young Patrick adopted journalism as a profession, and after a short experience on *The Scientific American,* he associated himself with his stepfather in the conduct of the *Irish American.* Under their care the paper rapidly grew in circulation and influence, and was soon looked up to as a guide and able champion by the Irish-Americans, not only of New York, but all over the country who found that their friends were then few and their foes many and powerful.

On the death of Mr. Lynch in May, 1857, Patrick Meehan succeeded to the chief editorial chair of the *Irish American,* a position which he retained to the day of his death. A leader in Irish-American affairs, social, political and religious, he was one of the first Catholics to serve on the Brooklyn Board of Education.

As a leading journalist, Patrick Meehan was naturally prominent in Irish-American politics. He kept the tone of his paper always conservative, and consistent to the fixed principles of Irish nationality.

When the Civil War broke out, and there was question as to how Irish-Americans should stand on the subject of secessions, Patrick Meehan strongly espoused the cause of the Union, and was prominently identified in enrolling the magnificent regiment of Irish soldiers who so gallantly conducted themselves during the subsequent disastrous conflicts. He was the intimate personal friend of Shields, Meagher, Corcoran, Cass, Guiney, Kelly, and other gallant soldiers who shed such imperishable lustre on the Irish name and largely helped them to organize the splendid bodies of men they commanded. He was much interested from his youth in military affairs, and in early manhood was a lieutenant in the 37th Irish Rifles, one of many Irish-American military organizations formed here after the Crimean War in the hope that the British crisis was the long-wished-for Irish opportunity. Later he served for a number of years as the senior captain of the Ninth Regiment of the New Jersey State Militia.

When at the close of the War, the Fenian Brotherhood began to develop, Patrick Meehan took stand among its leaders as his past services in the cause and ability justly entitled him to. He was elected member of the Senate of the organization and in July, 1865, in company with P. W. Dunne of Illinois, another member of the Senate, he was sent to Ireland to investigate the working of the organization there. He narrowly escaped arrest, and on his return to the United States in September of the same year, his report to the Philadelphia convention and the differences of policy with John O'Mahony, the Head Centre, were followed by the dissensions which split the great Fenian organizations into two sections, the followers of O'Mahony and those of President Roberts and the Senate. Identifying himself with latter, Patrick Meehan assumed the leadership of the organization. Unfortunately, how- ever, Patrick Meehan's conservatism and strict regard for honesty and justice brought him in conflict with men who schemes led to selfish and improper ends. On the night of February 28, 1870, as he and a party of other senators were leaving the Fenian head- quarters in West Fourth Street, a man whom he had befriended but who had enlisted himself with O'Mahony, came up behind him and shot him. The bullet entered just behind Patrick Meehan's right ear, where it remained to the day of his death. The tragic event proved the death blow to the organization; for, disheartened by the course its management had taken, the good men who had supplied its vitality left it, and the great Brotherhood in which so many hopes had been centered, and to the building up of which so many years of patient toil and sacrifice had been given, melted away in a few months without even a remnant to lag superfluous on the stage of Irish politics.

Patrick Meehan wrote copiously and vigorously, his style caustic and logical. Beside his journalistic work, he edited and prepared for the press a number of volumes of the "Irish-American Libra- ry," notably Father Burke's sermons and lectures, and the replies which both the eloquent Dominican and John Mitchell made to Froude's sophistries. He also compiled for many years the *Irish- American Almanac,* a valuable year book. In the early seventies he published the Gaelic class books without which the movement for the preservation of the old tongue of the Gael could not begin to make some progress here. The desire to revive the national language was no new fad even then, for as far back as 1857 he had the work in view, and as there was no Gaelic type in this country wherewith to begin the publication of a Gaelic Department in the *Irish American,* he ordered from London the dies and matrices necessary to cast a font of type in this city. Michael Doheny, John O'Mahony, Patrick O'Dea and other well known scholars of the time contributed to this department of the paper. One of the last acts of his long active career, which came to a close on April 29, 1906, was to look over the Gaelic matter printed in the last issue of the paper.[1]

Thomas Meehan's mother, Mary Jane Butler, a native of Ennis, County Clare, Ireland, came to this country with her mother in 1849, at the age of fourteen. On October 7, 1853, she and Patrick Meehan were married by the Rev. Eugene Cassidy in old St. James Cathedral, Brooklyn. They were among the founders of the Visitation Parish and later were members of the Star of the Sea Church on Court Street where Mrs. Meehan identified herself with parish interests and aided in everything that tended to its upbuilding. Her quiet unassuming manner endeared her to her fellow parishioners, as a gentle lady and a good Catholic mother.

Such was the heritage of Thomas Meehan. The family, at the time of his birth, lived on Nelson Street. When he was four years old, the Meehans, induced by the hope of greater prospects, moved to a new homestead on Jersey City Heights overlooking a panoramic picture of New York City and the Hudson River. The young couple showed their devout Catholicism by traveling five miles to the nearest church, that of St. Paul of the Cross in the adjoining village. Fifty years later, in 1904, as a tribute to their life of good example and fervent devotion, Bishop John J. O'Connor of Newark sent them permission to have the Golden Nuptial Mass celebrated in their own home, by the Reverend Frank J. Van Antwerp, of Detroit, Michigan, who was related to the Meehans.

2. EARLY DAYS

Thomas was the oldest of eleven children.[2] At an early age, he began his studies in a little French school near his Jersey home.

---

[1] *Irish American,* Dec. 18, 1909.

[2] The other children were Margaret, Mary, Joseph, Stephen, George, Nell, Pauline, Jane, Josephine and Frank. Two of the Butler children were brought up in the Meehan home.

CLASS OF 1873
College of St. Francis Xavier, New York
(Thomas F. Meehan is seated second from the right)

As soon as he was old enough to travel to New York, he was sent to Xavier High School at 30 West Sixteenth Street, New York City, where the Jesuit routine of scholastic studies kept the students busy all the day, strict attention being the rule and mere passive attendance the exception. Usually one professor taught all the subjects and in a very short time was intimate with all the students of his small class, twelve being considered a fair number. Thomas Meehan in his later years liked to recall the fact that every student felt the eyes of the professor upon him. Each boy was called upon to recite several times each class hour, and the time was unfortunately ample for question. Nor could glibness save the unlucky lad who was not prepared. It was a usual thing to be writing themes in Greek, Latin and English. In the occasional class debates the students argued whether Longfellow or Tennyson was the better poet; or whether the Iliad or Aeneid was the more representative classic.

After completing his secondary studies, Thomas began his college work at St. Francis Xavier's College receiving his Bachelor of Arts degree in 1873 and his Master's degree the year following. It was to those days that the Reverend John Wynne, S.J., referred when he said:

> "He was one of a class of young gentlemen to whom we beginners looked up, wondering if we could ever become like him. An impression still indelible is of their appearance when we were assembling for the College Mass on Saturday mornings. I recall some of the sermons we heard after the Mass, but the memory is by no means as vivid as the vision of decorum and reverence manifested by those Seniors and outstanding among them all was the gentle Meehan. He excelled in what the College prized most—deportment."

Three of Thomas Meehan's classmates were elevated to the ranks of the hierarchy: Right Reverend Charles E. McDonnell, Bishop of Brooklyn, Right Reverend James A. McFaul, Bishop of Trenton, Right Reverend Charles Henry Colton, Bishop of Buffalo. The class boasted of many priestly vocations: Reverend Charles F. Payten, Reverend Edward J. Conroy, Reverend Daniel J. McCormick, Reverend George A. Fargis, S.J., Reverend Joseph L. Hoey, of New York, and Reverend Jeremiah A. Brosnan and Reverend John McCloskey, of Brooklyn. Right Reverend Monsignor E. M. Sweeney, of Manhattan, also belonged to the class, but ill-health occasioned a lengthy absence and he was graduated in 1874. The laymen of the class were C. J. Sullivan, E. J. Mulvaney, W. H. McLean, James McGovern, Homer Nelson and Thomas F. Meehan. The only Brooklynite in the class was Thomas B. Murphy, later Principal of Public School No. 72, who like Monsignor Sweeney and the late Michael H. Curran, was graduated with '74. A class list of the early years includes the distinguished name of Hanselman. In the class of '72 which preceded them were three distinguished Brooklynites with whom Thomas Meehan formed sincere friendships to be strengthened with the ensuing years: Monsignor David J. Hickey, Monsignor Eugene F. Donnelly, and Mr. Andrew T. Sullivan.

In the "Bishop's Anniversay Number" supplement of *The Tablet* issued on the occasion of the Silver Jubilee of Bishop McDonnell, on April 25, 1917, Thomas Meehan wrote the following account of "The Bishop's School Days," which is a reflection of his own:

"The professor who had us in charge during our junior and sophomore years, the late Rev. Peter Cassidy, S.J., was a Brooklynite. He was what we would now style "a square man," in all his dealings with all his boys. We were attracted to him by his engaging personality, but his persuasive influence harmonized us all into a smoothly working fraternal group. One of his favorite admonitions used to be that we were to regard him as "our big brother Pete." For the future Bishop of Brooklyn he had a special affection and admiration, which were cordially reciprocated.

Bishop McDonnell entered the college in 1867, being enrolled in what was then called the Second Grammar Class. Modern pedagogy gives it a different title now, but the work done covers about the same ground. He followed the regular course until Summer of 1872, when he left New York for the American College, Rome, to take up there his theological studies. Monsignor Eugene Donnelly, of Flushing, was his trans-Atlantic companion then.

When, on the morning of March 11, 1892, we learned of the cable that announced his appointment as the second Bishop of Brooklyn, those of the alumni who lived in Brooklyn were delighted. On counting heads we found that we had representatives of twenty-five classes residing in the diocese. We held a meeting and invited the new bishop to let us welcome him at a strictly family gathering. He accepted and we gave him a fine dinner at the Clarendon, on the second evening of his career in Brooklyn, May 3, 1892. There were about one hundred former students of the college present, the only outsiders being the late Archbishop Corrigan, Bishop Chatard of Vincennes, who had ordained the new Bishop in Rome; the then Monsignor but later, Cardinal Farley, and Fathers May, Mitchel and Carroll as representatives of the priests of Brooklyn."

The vocational plans of most of Thomas Meehan's college associates seem to have centered largely upon the learned professions, but Thomas was ready to become associated with the newspaper world. Immediately after his graduation from Saint Francis Xavier's College, he became associated with the *Irish American* and then began that long journalistic career which made him a veritable "apostle of the press." His associates soon discovered in him those traits and characteristics which endeared him to his fellow workers. From his father he had inherited a love of detail, a great feeling for Irish history and a sense of humor. His mother seems to have given him her quiet gentleness of manner. Though she was exceptionally beautiful, it was her charming manner that made her a distinctive personality. Her children idolized her and Thomas was always proud of her. She influenced him profoundly in the formative years of his boyhood, and all through his years he owed to her the absence of formality, the dislike of standing on ceremony, and the spontaneous gift of warm and generous sympathy which won him such a host of friends.

3. MARRIAGE

When Thomas Meehan was twenty-eight years of age the Sunday *Democrat* of May 1, 1881, carried the following announcement of his marriage to Molly O'Rourke:

"On Thursday, April 28, at 5 o'clock P.M., Miss Molly O'Rourke was united in marriage to Mr. Thomas Meehan at St. Mary's Church, by the Rev. Charles Parks, in the presence of the pastor, Rev. Edward O'Reilly, and Father Smith of Jersey City, and a select company of friends. A reception followed at the residence of the bride's parents in Attorney Street, which was quite largely attended, the bride's father being Mr. P. O'Rourke who has been connected with the

Tribune for some thirty-five years and, of course, has hosts of friends. Mr. Meehan is the son of our respected Mr. Meehan, editor and proprietor of that notable sheet *Irish American,* and, as in duty bound, we offer our sincere congratulations, to the newly-wed couple. May their path of life lead to the joys of heaven."*

The Brooklyn Eagle (April 30, 1881) tells us that the friends who attended were:

". . . among the friends who witnessed the administration of the marriage rite were: Father Smith of St. Paul of the Cross, Hoboken, Fathers Philip, Meister and Isidore; the parents, aunts and sisters of the bride; Mr. and Mrs. and the Misses Meehan; Mr. Samuel Orchard and his wife; Colonel William R. Roberts; Major William L. Cole; wife, son and daughter, Judge Timothy Campbell and his reputed successor Counselor Michael H. Siggerson; Mrs. Michael Hennessey and son; Mr. and Mrs. J. Lalor; Mr. Thomas N. Rocker of the *Tribune;* and several others . . ."

The bride's father, Patrick O'Rourke, was born in the County Westmeath, 1814, and came to New York when about twenty-one years old. He settled in the Fourteenth Ward, and later moved into the Thirteenth Ward, in which he continued to reside until 1883, when he moved to Brooklyn. Early in his career he made the acquaintance of the late Horace Greeley, and a warm and lasting friendship grew up between the great journalist and the young Irishman with whom he differed so radically in religious and political opinions. They labored together through the publication of the *Log Cabin,* on the historical Harrison campaign, in 1840; and when, in 1841, that paper was succeeded by the *Daily Tribune,* Patrick O'Rourke became one of the stockholders, and took charge of the engineering department of the establishment. He assisted in getting out the first number of that paper, and was connected with it continuously up to the time of his death.[3]

4. CONTEMPORARY JOURNALISTS

Thomas Meehan was a born journalist, reveling in the various assignments of a reporter. In his younger days he was associated

---

*There were five children born to Thomas and Molly Meehan: Edward, John, Mary, Katherine, Pauline.

[3]The *Irish American,* December 26, 1885.

with men who had known the great men in the generation before them. His story might well be called a record of famous friendships. The period was full of names now famous in the pages of American thought.

When Father Hecker founded the Congregation of Saint Paul and the Congregation began to publish the *Catholic World,* a new light seemed to dawn. Here, for the first time, there appeared to be an effort to bring the Catholic Church in America into relation with what might be called, in the best sense, "Americanism."

There was the beginning of a great Catholic movement, a chance to take a step forward in the evolution of Catholic literature of which Mrs. Sadlier, Richard Watson Gilder, and Dr. Huntington were the principal interpreters; Orestes Brownson was then alive and the survivors of the Brook Farm experiment were still arguing their famous point. To this era belonged also Charles Anderson Dana,[4] whom some looked upon as an oracle. At this time the field was very fertile for young writers.

A life-long friend of Thomas Meehan's was Maurice Francis Egan, a man prominent in his own day, who was born May 24, 1852. His father was a Tipperary man who in 1880 married Katherine Mullen of Philadelphia. At this time, the *Freeman's Journal,* which had been a power, was fast declining. Like all important periodicals of that time it felt the change in the public attitude toward personal journalism. Interest in "editorials" was waning; news was becoming more important. Henry Watterson still held his old prestige, but with the exception of Mr. Dana, nobody really cared what any other editor thought,[5] even if the editor was Horace Greeley.

Maurice Francis Egan's chief at this time was James McMaster, a rabid states-rights Democrat and anti-abolitionist in politics. His fierce assaults on President Lincoln and his administration resulted in his being arrested in 1861 and confined for some time

---

[4]After the failure of Brook Farm, Charles Anderson Dana became associated with the *New York Tribune.* Because of his editorial "On to Richmond," and his disagreement with Horace Greeley in war politics, he was forced to resign. Later he became chief editor of the *New York Sun* which position he held until his death.

[5]Egan's—"Recollections of a Happy Life," p. 126.

in Fort Lafayette as a disloyal citizen. The paper was suppressed by the Government and did not resume publication until April 19, 1862. A milder tone was adopted as far as national politics went.

James McMaster was always the strong and valuable champion of the rights of the Holy See and of Catholic schools. The lash of his fiercest vituperation was plied upon those who would compromise in the least way the principle of religious education. We of this generation can hardly realize the force and influence of what in the old times was known as "personal journalism," the kind that depended for its weight on the individual man who was the editorial writer of the paper.

With another generation and new ideals, people tired of McMaster's literary violence, and his prestige waned. "I used to see him often," says Thomas Meehan, "during his last years as Egan and I were together almost daily and I got to be a favorite as I was a good listener and he loved to relate his adventures."[6]

Maurice Francis Egan became McMaster's associate in 1880. His brilliant and attractive style gave a spicy flavor to the editorial page of the *Freeman's Journal*, but his style was hampered by the whims and eccentricities of the aged and sickly McMaster.[7]

After McMaster's death, on December 29, 1886, Maurice Francis Egan acquired from the estate a half proprietorship of the paper,[8] which he successfully conducted alone until the middle of the year 1888 when it was purchased by the Fords.[9] In 1894 the new owners made Reverend Louis Lambert the editor.

Egan went to Notre Dame in 1888 to fill the chair of English Literature, remaining there until 1896, when he took the same position at the Catholic University of America. In 1907 he resigned his professorship on his appointment as Minister to Denmark by President Theodore Roosevelt and later confirmed by Presidents Taft and Wilson, resigning because of ill health in 1918. President Cleveland previously had offered him the mission to Greece, which he declined. Promotion to the ambassadorship at Vienna from Copenhagen was tendered by Presidents Taft and

---

[6]Letter to Reverend Peter Guilday, May 28, 1926.
[7]*Catholic News,* April 11, 1908.
[8]*Freeman's Journal,* Volume L, February 25, 1888.
[9]*Freeman's Journal,* Volume L, August 4, 1888.

Wilson and also declined. The only other public office he held was as a member of the Indian Commission (1906-1907).

Thomas Meehan's daughter Molly was bridesmaid at the marriage of Maurice Egan's daughter Patricia in Copenhagen. The ceremony took place at St. Ansgar's in the Bredgade, recognized as the diplomatic Church since the greater part of the envoys to Copenhagen were Catholics. According to Monseigneur von Fuch, Patricia's marriage was the first celebrated by Nuptial Mass since the Reformation.

In "Ten Years Near the German Frontier" (Doran, 1919), Dr. Egan told the story of his diplomatic experience. The volume had an instantaneous and widespread popular success. When he returned home after an absence of eleven years he found that most of his old social and literary intimates had passed away. His great life is told in his autobiography "Recollections of a Happy Life." This was edited by Thomas Francis Meehan who was Maurice Egan's literary executor. Henry Van Dyke who wrote the foreword calls it "a delectable book."

One incident that Egan relates is:

"Another promising young man at that time was Conde Pallen, who belonged to St. Louis. His father, Dr. Montrose Pallen, had an exquisite set of tapestries, made for Marie DeMedici. Conde was much under the influence of his mother's people who were French and who, being a part of the history of St. Louis, were almost more French than the Parisians themselves. It was a great pleasure to see him in New York, and we always tried to give him a party. Shortly after my marriage, in the summer when my wife had gone to Cape May with her relatives, I tried one of these parties on my own account. The maid had gone. It was in the heat of the summer and difficult to borrow or hire another servant. I had invited the guests to come to our apartment without considering the difficulties. As it was early July I managed to procure some enormous strawberries and a can of Devonshire cream which an unhappy Englishman had tried to introduce into Brooklyn. He had a place for a short time on Fulton Street. And then there was to be ice cream and cake and something to drink. At the last moment I discovered that the silver with the exception of what the waiters call a "cover for one" had been locked up. I remember that William S. Walsh of the *Herald* and the delectable David Munro, then of *Harper's*, and Thomas F. Meehan were to be of the assembly. Mrs. Munro was away in the country. The maid somehow failed—telephones were rare in those days. I managed to secure enough glasses for the punch, but the strawberries and the ices were a problem. When the guests arrived, I could offer them only wooden toothpicks for the strawberries. It went very well, but some malignant creature wafted the story to my wife and I was reminded many times of the act which she had considered entirely inexcusable.

In fact the only excuse I had for some of my strange parties was that I loved to give them, and the absence of my wife, who was rather conventional in the Philadelphia way, gave me full liberty for hospitable agility. Jim Huneker was a real ornament to these bachelor affairs. Sometimes he brought friends who had to be explained; but they always added to the gaiety of the occasion."[10]

James Huneker was one who even in his youthful days horrified the orthodox by quoting from recondite books which were looked upon as diabolical. This was, of course, before he went to the Conservatory of Paris; he was already dominated by French literature and the influence of German music. In Europe he was looked on as among the first of American critics, and his opinion of the theatrical side of the opera was highly regarded.[11]

Thomas Meehan's days on the newspapers, or I should say his nights, were so regulated that he could find an hour or two during the opera season to listen to his favorite singers. He was a great friend of William Guard, Press agent of the Metropolitan, who much to his own delight strongly resembled Robert Louis Stevenson. Interviewing the great of his period was one of Thomas Meehan's particularly congenial tasks, and he was an inveterate "first nighter" at the opera, as well as at all the dramatic performances of his era. His prodigious memory enshrined a multitude of stars. It was a privilege to go to the Opera or theatre with him, for between the acts, he could learn the history of every performer and all his great achievements, as well as many an interesting and revealing story.[12] He knew what was worth knowing and he knew it well.

---

[10]Egan's—"Recollections of a Happy Life," p. 143.
[11]Egan's—"Recollections of a Happy Life," p. 364.
[12]Cornelia Craigie.

5. LITERARY ENDEAVORS

Thomas Meehan was one of that group who organized the Fenelon Reading Circle, a literary organization established under the direction of Bishop McDonnell to foster and cultivate a taste for reading—Catholic in teaching and tone. The members were indirectly interested in historical work. When commenting on it in later years, Thomas Meehan said:

"We started the Fenelon thirty odd years ago when the 'Reading Circle' idea was rife, and kept it going for several years on a high class literary and social plane (this was during the first years of Bishop McDonnell's administration). Then the founders, as in most societies, got tired and let the management go to others."[13]

The organization is still active today under the direction of Reverend Joseph A. Murphy, D.D.

The Catholic Writers' Guild, another of Thomas Meehan's favorite projects, was organized by Patrick Cardinal Hayes, at the instance of Dr. John Talbot Smith,[14] at a meeting held at the archepiscopal residence on December 12, 1919. Because of his encouragement, sound advice and tireless efforts, Thomas Meehan was chosen its first President. In November, 1920, he resigned because he felt that it was not possible for him to give the duties of the office the attention that the activities of the Guild required. The purposes of this Guild are to promote the interests of writers and help them in the attainment of their aspirations, to afford them the opportunity of mutual acquaintance and appreciation through association and correspondence, to create and maintain a spirit of cordial understanding between the Church and the Press; to challenge all articles or pronouncements derogatory to religion by letters of protest to press, screen, stage and radio; to use the united influence of its members to establish a spirit of good-will toward all creeds and races; to make this nation of ours "A More United States."

Since its organization hundreds of writers and persons interested in literary work have become members of the Guild, among them many outstanding literateurs. Right Reverend Fulton J.

---

[13]Letter to Monsignor Guilday, March 5, 1928.
[14]*New Catholic Dictionary*, p. 1027.

Sheen, Thomas Woodlock, Kenton Kilmer, and others, are among the members who govern this association today.

It will be recalled that upon his graduation from College, Thomas Meehan began immediately to devote his life to the press. His services were in demand as correspondent for newspapers throughout the country. In fact, he was one of the first to get an entree into the secular press for items of Catholic interest. His friends recall how eagerly his daily letter to the *Baltimore Sun* was read by people who knew little of New York. He was New York correspondent of the *Baltimore Sun,* 1888-1895, and for the *Philadelphia Public Ledger,* 1898-1905, the *Richmond Times* (Va.) and for *De Massabode,* Rotterdam, Holland. He also served on the editorial staff of the *New York Herald* from 1895-1897, and was a special contributor to the *New York Sun, New York Star, The Brooklyn Eagle* and *The Brooklyn Citizen.*

His quiet, gentle manner never changed, even in trying positions. Once, particularly, when he was unjustly treated by one in high position and for whom he had done favors, he remained unruffled, though he felt the injury done him and was deeply wounded by the fact that those who caused the injury should be so untrue to their profession. The experience proved to be a blessing in disguise, as now after thirty years in secular journalism, he was available at last for important work in Catholic publications. The manager of the *Catholic Encyclopedia* welcomed Thomas Meehan as manager of their editorial rooms shortly after that great work was begun in 1905.

A brief reference of the details of the progress made in the compilation of the *Catholic Encyclopedia* is not without interest now. The idea took its inception from a long article printed in the *Messenger Magazine* for June 1902, in which the editor, the Reverend John J. Wynne, S.J., drew attention to the injustice done, in treating Catholics and kindred subjects in the most important of the general encyclopedias, appealing for public patronage. After a careful consideration of the scheme, it was then determined that publication of the *Catholic Encyclopedia,* in English, was one of the imperative needs of the time.

Intending to present its readers with the full body of Catholic teaching, the editors determined that each article should be prepared and signed by the ablest available writer. To secure these contributions the bishops in the English speaking countries and heads of Religious Orders and Congregations and of Catholic Universities, Colleges and Seminaries were communicated with for suggestions.

No other work has ever been produced by the labor of so many Catholic men and women, an army of contributors making a concrete showing of the intellectual developments of the Church. In the words of Georges Goyau, the project was "a modern intellectual crusade."

Thomas F. Meehan's newspaper training made him the ideal man for the job, and in the shortest possible time he had endeared himself to everyone by his kindness and his patience. These qualities were needed, for most of the copy-readers were not professionals. His sense of humor seemed aroused by their difficulties. As the very foremost authority on American Catholic history, he was of immense value to the Editors of the *Catholic Encyclopedia.* He actively supervised the first five volumes and wrote a great number of articles for the entire fifteen volumes. He is said to have written more articles for it than any other person. A look at the list of articles he wrote will give a fair idea of the vast store of knowledge that was his.[15] He had a prodigious memory, for he seldom had to refer to books to clinch an argument. He was very familiar with the history of the Church, past and contemporary, and so very efficient at what is now styled "public relations" activity. How he amassed his knowledge about affairs of interest to Catholics was always a matter of surprise, but more surprising still was his memory of it all. "Delightful also was the modesty with which he imparted it. With him it was not history, but the very life of the Church."[16]

The final volume of the *Catholic Encyclopedia* compiled under the editorial management and direction of Dr. Blanche M. Kelly, is the key to the whole contents and without it the research and marvelous resources of the encyclopedia would not be available on demand. She joined the editorial staff of the Encyclopedia in 1907, after completing her studies at Kenwood. Others of her editorial associates of the staff who deserve special mention for

---

[15]See list in the Appendix.
[16]Rev. John J. Wynne, S.J.

the important and scholarly work they did in preparing the contents of the several volumes for publication were the late Ewan Macpherson, an indefatigable worker overflowing with the versatile information most needed for such publication; the late Florence M. Rudge, editor and member of the first class graduated at Trinity College; Eugene F. Saxton, late president of Harper Brothers; the late James Gray, literary editor of the *New York Sun;* Cornelia Craigie, Mrs. Josephine Donovan, Joseph O'Rourke, Thomas Woodlock, a life long friend of Thomas Meehan, Leo Kelly and Andrew McErlean.

Thomas F. Meehan's interest in the members of the staff went far beyond their office work. His kind and valuable advice and active assistance in their extra-Encyclopedia literary aspirations was never wanting. He was patient in argument, but persistent. He kept well-ordered files of valuable papers and clipping that came to his notice. If asked for information on his favorite subject he produced in a few moments a packet of data that would be a mine of information to the would-be writer or research worker. He could get a whole saga out of a dusty little fact that others would not have noticed. It was interesting to walk through the streets with him and listen while he called back to life the dead who once walked those streets and who once lived in those adjoining houses. One could discuss a subject with him on three or four occasions and on the fifth, discover a bright jewel of information, withheld till then. What an enormous charm there is in such a mind, which thus always has the power to surprise!

It is not surprising to find Thomas Meehan giving his wholehearted cooperation, his able assistance and his every effort to the great enterprise of the *Catholic Builders of the Nation.*

The editors of the *Catholic Builders of the Nation* realized that no complete survey could be made of the work of Catholics in the building up of the material life and the professional cultural ideals of this nation. Obviously the scantiness of records makes any approximation to completeness quite out of the question. Nevertheless, it was relatively easy to present some notion of the significance of their contribution to the development of the civilization of this republic through the judicious selection of typical characters and events.[17]

---

[17]*Catholic Builders of the Nation*—foreword by Admiral Wm. S. Benson, LL.D., Volume I, pp. 12-13.

It was with this end in view that the *Catholic Builders of the Nation* was published. The editors aimed to bring together a number of aspects of Catholic activity—to show that the part taken by those of the Catholic Faith has been an honorable, deserving and indispensable one in the building up of the nation. The work is a symposium of Catholic contributions to the civilization of the United States. Thomas Meehan was one of its editors and contributor of the following articles:

"Catholic New York," Volume I, pp. 251-267
"Wartime Ministering Angels," Volume III, pp. 276-296
"Catholic Pioneer Captains of Industry," Volume III, pp. 161-174
"The Catholic Press," Volume IV, pp. 219-234

6. OTHER ACTIVITIES

Among the many interests which engrossed the attention of our busy journalist was the problem of the Indian missions. In 1904, Reverend Father Ganss, a priest of very unusual ability and culture, who had dedicated his ministry to the cause of Catholic Indians, came to New York to plead for the safeguarding of our faith among the Indians. His magnificent work for the poor, afflicted and the abandoned commended itself highly to the charity workers of all creeds in our country. Under the leadership of Father Ganss, Thomas Mulry immediately enlisted in the cause and by his influence gathered together prominent members of the St. Vincent de Paul Society thus forming the nucleus of the Marquette League. By their liberality, zeal and wisdom, they laid the foundation of the organization which was soon incorporated under the laws of the State of New York to work for the interests of the Catholic Indians in this country, and to serve as an adjunct of the society for the Propagation of the Faith by rendering financial aid to Catholic missionaries working among the thousands of unconverted Indians in this country.[18]

The activities of the League started under the direction of Edward Eyre, President; Thomas Minahan, Vice-President; Theodore E. Tack, Treasurer; Joseph P. Grace, Secretary; and Reverend Henry Ganss, Thomas Mulry and Judge Eugene Phil-

---

[18]*Catholic News*, May 7, 1904.

bin, Directors.[19] From the year after its organization until his death Thomas Meehan served as a member of the Board of Directors.

During the years that he was associated with the League he was deeply interested in the missionary labors of the priests and Sisters who were spreading the Gospel of Christ among the American Indians.[20] Nor was this interest greater than that which manifested itself in the work of the Church at home. In his work with the St. Vincent de Paul Society, he became closely associated with Thomas Mulry, who has been not inaptly styled the "American Ozanam." Only a short time previously Mulry had been elected the head of the reorganized St. Vincent de Paul Society of the United States, with the title of President of its Superior Council. He had a national reputation as the foremost Catholic layman in the field of charitable activities as well as in the financial world. He was born in New York City, February 13, 1855. His family moved to the West in 1862 and remained there 10 years. When he returned to New York he engaged in the contracting business with his father. In 1901, he was elected a trustee of the Emigrant Industrial Savings Bank and became its president in 1906. He was progressive and wise. His integrity, wisdom and charity were known to all. The poor trusted him completely and he was known as a just man throughout the nation. In 1908, Pope Pius X created him a Knight of the Order of St. Gregory and in 1912 he received the Laetare Medal from Notre Dame for ". . . his heroic devotion to works of charity extending over a quarter of a century." While engaged in large business enterprises and acting president of a large banking house he devoted half his time for relief of suffering humanity. He died at his residence at 10 Perry Street in New York City on March 10, 1916.

The life of Thomas Mulry was the only book that Thomas Meehan ever wrote. A review in the *Catholic Historical Review* says:

---

[19]Jubilee Sermon of Right Reverend Monsignor John P. Chidwick, D.D., printed in the *Calumet*, May 1929.

[20]Resolutions adopted by Bd. of Directors M. L.—July 7, 1942, Reverend Bernard Cullen, Dir. Gen.—Victor Ridder, Pres.

"Not the least valuable part of this book consists in the selection of speeches delivered on various important occasions by Mr. Mulry. . . . The only criticism we can offer is that the biography is entirely too brief to do justice to his memory, and adequately portray his lifelong activity in charitable works."[21]

The book was written under the pressure of many other duties, and does not do justice to the historical acumen of its devoted author.

Everyone who knew Thomas Meehan wondered why he did not publish more. He had contributed to magazines, Catholic and secular, to year-books, to encyclopedias; he had written prefaces for many books which he had edited or revised. The editors of *America,* Reverend R. H. Tierney, S.J., Father Parson and Father Talbot, were continually urging him to write his autobiography. That would have been a book of real value, but he never seemed to welcome the idea. The unfortunate modesty of a true scholar made him believe that the book would be worthless.

The nearest approach to such a book was a beautifully bound volume of blank pages presented by him to Mrs. Thomas McGoldrick. The title page was inscribed:

MY BOOK
Being the
MEMOIRS, ADVENTURES and
RECOLLECTIONS OF
A GAY YOUNG
BLADE OF
'78
(limited edition)
NEW YORK
1933
(Autographed) to R. C. M.
with the devoted
homage of the author.
T. F. M.
St. Valentine's Day
1933

---

[21]*Catholic Historical Review,* Sept. 1917, p. 288.

7. His Writings

Any true picture of the life that spanned so grandly the history of Catholicity growing great in America should include a panoramic view of Thomas Meehan's writings during the several decades of his untiring devotion to the cause.

The celebration of the centenary of the erection of the See of New York gave him an opportunity to follow, in a series of historical sketches, many hitherto neglected bypaths of Catholic life and interest.

His "Publishers and Booksellers—Barclay Street,"[22] was one of this series; but he had treated the subject years before in the *Brooklyn Citizen*[23] under the title of "Pater Noster Row—The Curious Phase of New York Life That Is Called the Publishing Business."

Over a period from 1886 to 1897 he contributed to the *Brooklyn Eagle, The Citizen,* and the *New York Herald* innumerable articles in which he sketched the history of the Brooklyn parishes, listing meticulously the names of all the clergy who labored there. These articles he later summarized for *The Catholic Church in America,* of which book he was co-editor.[24]

Local cemeteries were a pet province of Thomas Meehan's antiquarian muse. Included in the Centenary series was a group entitled "The Graves of the Dead," in which he studied in turn St. Paul's, St. Patrick's, The Old Eleventh Street Cemetery, and Calvary.

A letter which he wrote to the editor of *America*[25] in 1916, after a visit to Calvary, is eloquent of the delight he took in bringing to public notice again some Catholic notable long since forgotten:

"As I was wandering through Calvary Cemetery on Memorial Day, I stumbled on a plot that was the very picture of neglect, in one of the best sites of that silent city of a million Catholic dead. The grave is covered with a rank growth of weeds and grass; the fencing is thick with rust; the top

---

[22]*Catholic News,* March 28, 1908.

[23]*Brooklyn Citizen,* June 12, 1887.

[24]*The Catholic Church in the United States,* Volume III, "General History of Brooklyn," pp. 525-619, The Catholic Editing Company, N. Y., 1914.

[25]*America,* June 11, 1916.

of the once imposing shaft 'erected to the memory of Patrick Sarsfield Casserly' is broken.

"Patrick Casserly came to New York from Ireland in 1824 and was one of our first Catholic classical schoolmasters. He was an editor of the *Weekly Register,* and a contributor to the *Truth Teller,* two of our earliest Catholic papers, and edited several Greek and Latin text-books held in high repute and used for several generations in our schools. A curious advertisement in the *Truth Teller* of 1828 reads:

Chrestomathic Institution or Seminary for General Education, No. 36 Cherry Street, a few doors from Franklin Square. P. S. Casserly, T.C.D., Principal.

A select Female School has been established at Mr. Casserly's residence No. 6 Pell Street, next door to the Bowery, under the superintendence of experienced Ladies, one of whom will teach French and Music in a superior style. They will also have the assistance of the Masters employed in the Institution.

"Among his pupils was his son Eugene, who was admitted to the Bar in 1844 and served as New York's Corporation Attorney, 1846-1847. Like his father he was connected with early Catholic Journalism as one of the first editors of the *Freeman's Journal.* In 1850 he went to San Francisco where he took rank at once as a leading Democrat and was elected to the United States Senate from California in 1869. He died June 14, 1883. Another son, Bernard, was for years a member of the State Commission of Immigration. The mother of these two was one of the teaching staff of the 'Chrestomathic Institution' and a relative of Father Luke Berry, first pastor of St. Mary's Church, Grand Street.

"The National Convention of the Catholic Press Association is soon to meet in this city. It might not be an inappropriate detail of its proceedings to try and collect the few pennies necessary to make presentable this neglected memorial to one of the pioneers of the local Catholic press."

This note attracted wide attention. In response to a public desire for more details about Casserly and his great Institution, Thomas Meehan gave further details in "An Old Fashioned Teacher" printed in the *Catholic News,* November 25, 1916.

This is but one of the many instances in which Thomas Meehan's scholarly devotion to the past caused a renewed interest in the deeds of one who had long since been forgotten.

In a letter to Monsignor Peter Guilday, dated May 9, 1940, Thomas Meehan wrote:

". . . Yesterday, I spent more than an hour at the Office of Calvary Cemetery where I had gone to make the necessary arrangements for the 'perpetual care' (fee $500.00) of my future residence there. One of the much needed reforms recently has been better and more intelligent care of the Cemeteries. If I could cut 40 or 50 off my 86 record and tramp through, what a 'thesis' I could write about indifference to general unkempt conditions, and the sad state of the last resting place of so many 'prominents,' 'famous,' 'distinguished,' etc., in spite of the few dollars it would take to make them decent. Andrew Morris is buried in old St. Patrick's graveyard yet no one knows where, in spite of the fact that he was the most affluent Catholic in New York, the first to hold elective public office, Father Kohlman's intimate friend and reliance, practical builder of St. Patrick's, friend and host of Archbishop Caroll, local banker, etc., etc., etc."

Religious Communities are indebted to Thomas Meehan for his painstaking research in the field of pioneer labors such as those of Mother Seton of the Sisters of Charity and Mother Aloysia Hardey of the Madames of the Sacred Heart. The Sisters of Providence owe to him many of their records of the travels of Mother Theodore Guerin.

Families prominent in the early history of New York found in him their devoted historian: The New York Emmets, The Stoughtons, The Pardow Family, The Parmentiers of Brooklyn; and also, Lorenzo de Ponte, Doctor Henry James Anderson, MacNeven and countless others.

Eminent Churchmen like Archbishop Hughes, Cardinal McCloskey, Father Raffeiner, were always a subject of fascination for this indefatigable browser among old records.

"New York's 'Lily of Churches' and Archbishop Hughes" was printed the *Republic,* October 1, 1910. "Archbishop Hughes and Mexico" in Volume XIX, *Records and Studies.* The *Catholic Messenger* of Worcester, Massachusetts, reprinted in April, 1910, "The First American Cardinal" which had appeared in the *Catholic World* the previous month.

The apologetic value of publicity was early recognized by Thomas Meehan. His "A Hundred Years of the Roman Catholic Church in New York City" was published in the *Brooklyn Eagle* on April 28, 1908, and an explanation of "The Organization of the Catholic Church in the United States" appeared in the Novem-

ber 1908 issue of both the *North American Review* and the
Monitor.

For the Silver Jubilee edition of the *Tablet* in 1933 Thomas
Meehan wrote on "Catholic Journalism in New York City." Since
he was closely connected with the early Catholic papers of the
city, this topic had a special appeal for him. "Pioneers of the
Catholic Press" was written for *America*[26] and "Early Catholic
Weeklies" for *Records and Studies;*[27] "The First Catholic Monthly Magazine" was also for *Record and Studies.*[28]

The esteem in which Thomas Meehan was held in the opinion
of the staff of the *Brooklyn Eagle* is shown by the graciousness
with which the columnist John Heffernan replied to a rebuke
for him on a matter of inaccuracy about a point of Catholic
history:

"BOWING TO A SUPERIOR AUTHORITY"

May I delve into the litter of letters on my overburdened
writing table? Commendation and condemnation, as usual.
Here is one from that noted veteran journalist and historian,
Thomas F. Meehan, gently chiding me for a fault of memory.
The fault was mine, using the name of John McCloskey for
the man who supervised the digging of the trenches of the
Navy Yard. Says Mr. Meehan, and he is an authority:

"As a part of your Lenten penance, I am afraid you'll have
to revise your personal recollections of the family of the first
American Cardinal. Cardinal Farley, who among others, may
be accepted as a fairly good authority, wrote the life of Cardinal McCloskey, and in it, he says that Patrick McCloskey,
and his wife Eliza Harron McCloskey, the Cardinal's parents,
came to Brooklyn from the County Derry in 1808. He was
a farmer in Ireland, and got the job of gardener for the
Pierrepont property on the Heights, living in a cottage on
the property where the future Cardinal was born, March 20,
1810. Tradition says his mother could not nurse him, so, in
spite of a stormy night, Mrs. Pierrepont, who then had a
young baby, left the Mansion and went to the cottage and
attended to the needs of the newborn McCloskey. Several
years later the McCloskey's moved across the river to Murray
Street, New York, where Mr. McCloskey died in 1820. That
he was a 'builder' is a new phase of his record. When Fort

---

[26]*America,* March 16, 1935.
[27]*Records and Studies,* Volume XXVIII, pp. 237-255.
[28]*Records and Studies,* Volume XXXI, pp. 137-144.

Greene was thrown up in 1812, he bossed a squad of Pierre-pont workers who dug up the trenches."[29]

Thomas Meehan's historical writings had many angles. While he was writing and reviewing he kept his eye on reviewers as well. In the December 14, 1912, issue of *America* we find him reminding Henry Garrity, the writer of the foreword of "My Un-known Chum" by "Aguecheek" that one Charles Bullard had written a series of essays for the *Boston Evening Gazette* over the pen name of "Aguecheek."

In the course of his researches, Thomas Meehan's interests spread over a broad field. When discussing the work with Negroes he wrote:

"... This advertisement can be read in the files of the *New York Gazette:* 'Ran away the 18th of August, 1733, from Jacobus Van Cortlandt, of the City of New York, a negro slave named Andrew Saxton—the shirts he had with him and on his back are marked with a cross on the left breast. He professeth himself to be a Roman Catholic; speaks very good English. ..."[30]

He sought to preserve all data of this type and also that which had any anti-Catholic trends. He sent a whole collection of anti-Catholic literature of the "Maria Monk" character to St. Joseph's Seminary at Dunwoodie to be preserved there in an "alcove" devoted to historical research material. Referring to this, he said, "The Society's[31] 'alcove' is turning out better than we expected. I am sorry we did not think of it earlier and begin the work of saving much that has been lost in the vicissitudes of families."[32]

This phase of his work was commended by Cardinal Hayes:

"I am very much pleased with the new work that your fine scholarship is bringing to the attention of the Church in America. We are indeed blessed in your long, intelligent, and scholarly devotion to the interests of Church history.

"I am also grateful to learn that the 'alcove' at Dunwoodie is proving such a satisfying experiment."[33]

---

[29]*Brooklyn Daily Eagle,* by John Heffernan, February 11, 1940.
[30]*The Catholic Mind,* Volume XX, No. 8, April 22, 1922.
[31]This refers to the United States Catholic Historical Society.
[32]Letter from T. F. M. to Cardinal Hayes, November 13, 1932.
[33]Letter from Cardinal Hayes to T. F. M.

Thomas Meehan's native borough of Brooklyn was the child of predilection, naturally, when local ecclesiastical history was concerned. Its pre-Diocesan days were as familiar to him as were the days of Bishop Loughlin, of his classmate Bishop McDonnell and of his friend of later years, Bishop Molloy.

He contributed parish histories for countless journals, and pamphlets, and gave willing and cheerful assistance to students who were in quest of historical material. In 1913 he prepared a detailed account of St. James parish and revised it for its Centenary Journal in 1922. The fruits of his careful study of early records and his curious reading of the tombstones in the old graveyard on Jay Street are preserved for us in "A Village Churchyard,"[34] in "Cradle of Brooklyn Still Stands at York and Gold Streets—First Mass in 1822,"[35] "Early Landmarks Vanish with the March of Time,"[36] "Cradle of Catholic Brooklyn,"[37] "Catholic Brooklyn, a Century Ago,"[38] "Brooklyn."[39]

Public recognition of Thomas Meehan's various contributions to the history of the early days of Brooklyn came in 1911, when Mayor Gaynor appointed him a trustee of the Brooklyn Public Library to fill the vacancy left by the death of William D. Sargent, August 10, 1911.[40] By education and professional training Thomas Meehan was well equipped to deal with every question which came before the Board.

Among the pioneer Catholic families with which Thomas Meehan kept in contact were the Parmentiers of horticultural and philanthropic fame. Rosine Parmentier had the warmest regard for Thomas Meehan, who often visited her to talk of the early days of the Church in New York City and its vicinity, when her parents had to cross the river to attend Mass in old St. Peter's in Barclay Street.

It was at times like these that he gleaned so many of the interesting stories that made him the connecting link between "then

---

[34]*Records and Studies,* Volume VII.
[35]*Brooklyn Daily Eagle,* September 29, 1918.
[36]*Brooklyn Daily Eagle,* November 3, 1918.
[37]*The Tablet,* April 21, 1934.
[38]*The Tablet,* November 1, 1941.
[39]*Records and Studies,* Volume XXI.
[40]*Brooklyn Citizen,* September 1, 1911.

and now." It was Rosine's delight to tell of the old French
missionaries who used to visit the old home in Bridge Street.
When the famous Madame de Gallitzin landed here from France
en route to New Orleans in 1840, she stayed at the Parmentier
home. Bishop Dubois,[41] Father De Smet, S.J., Father Felix
Varela, Mother Theodore Guerin, Father Sorin and Cornelius
Heeney were among those who shared the hospitality of this
family.

The tribute paid to Thomas Meehan by a contemporary, beloved of Brooklynites for his own courageous defense of the
rights of the Church, is typical of the esteem in which his native
borough held him.

The Right Reverend Monsignor John L. Belford wrote of
Thomas Meehan in his *Mentor*:

"For more than sixty years he has been a shining light and
a tower of strength in Brooklyn. He sought not the notice and
praise of men. He gave all his time and all his ability to
diffuse the truth, to promote justice and this to do, in these
days what God sent His Son to do in days gone by—to make
God known and loved. With the eyes of a prophet and the
enthusiasm of an apostle, he saw the birth and the growth of
the Church in Brooklyn. The Lord blessed him with His
choicest gifts, long life, deep faith and great talent. These he
used with the generosity which charity inspired. He lived
and worked for the glory of God and the welfare of his
brethren. He had not patience with the Catholic, cleric or layman, whose ignorance or vanity made him 'broad' and let
him into the swamp of popularity by criticising or defying
ecclesiastical authority. What a pity men like Mr. Meehan
cannot bequeath the knowledge they have acquired in patience
and in toil! They can leave their property and their name,
but they cannot leave what is far more precious—their knowledge."[42]

---

[41]Note: Bishop Dubois spent two days every week in the Parmentier
home, to administer the affairs of the Church in Brooklyn before the Diocese was established.

[42]*The Mentor*, by Right Reverend Monsignor John L. Belford, August,
1942.

8. "Masses Apppreciated"

Not the least among Thomas Meehan's contributions to the richness of Catholic life throughout the United States was the practice of inserting in death notices a request for Masses.

When on September 10, 1916, after a very brief illness, his beloved wife died, the true and Christ-like spirit of Thomas Meehan was made manifest. Here, the full radiance of that hidden and supernatural life shone forth. He was eloquent, not with his tongue but with his pen; that pen, "he wielded with the skill of a swordsman and the strength of a giant, but always with the conscience of a Christian and the gentleness of one who loved his fellowmen."[43] It had marvelous power and it had great simplicity as is shown when he had the following notice inserted into the local newspaper:

Meehan. Mary O'Rourke, wife of Thomas F. Meehan, 205 Greene Avenue, Brooklyn; Requiem Thursday, September 12, 1916, at 10 o'clock, Queen of All Saints Chapel. Masses would be appreciated.

It was a simple sentence of four words: "Masses would be appreciated." What more evidence of genuine Catholicity than that? It was the first time that such an expression appeared in a newspaper and the Catholic weeklies were not slow to point out this beautiful example for imitation by all Catholics. *The Lamp* for November 1916 commented:

"There was a certain novelty about such an expression appearing in the public press which gave us much food for thought. This was indeed a return to the old time Faith of our fathers—to those days which find an echo in the inscriptions in the old Roman catacombs. For once upon a time it was the usual thing to remember one's deceased friends with Masses rather than with flowers."

It is a common thing today to read in an obituary notice "Masses appreciated." Few, however, know that it was Thomas Meehan who was the first to use it.

Maurice Francis Egan, LL.D., U. S. Minister Plenipotentiary to Denmark and a very close friend of the Meehan family wrote this poem upon the death of Mrs. Meehan.

---

[43]*The Mentor,* by Right Reverend Monsignor John L. Belford, August, 1942.

"IN MEMORIAM"

Thou hast a sting, O Death, a hateful sting,
(But Grave, thou cans't not claim the Victory,
Since He, Our Lord, arose to Life through Thee),
Dark Shade, thy coming changes everything
That makes our little joys; thy bells that ring
Drown all sweet, earthly sounds; on land and sea
More sad or fearful music cannot be
Or sight than the swift-sweeping of thy wing.
From us that happiness passes through the door
When she went out; in Spring the violet
Is not the same; the lighted street at eve
Before her home;—no more, no more, no more
The welcome of her smile. My eyes are wet:—
I know, O Lord, I know; but I must grieve.

9. HIS CORRESPONDENCE

Thomas Meehan led a comparatively quiet life. One of his antipathies was the empty chatter of social life, the insignificant talk that simply wastes time. He considered time the essence of life, man's once priceless, fleeting possession that, once spent, can never be regained. He worked assiduously and lovingly without ostentation. He was ever amused at the increasing complexity of life that kept everyone ceaselessly active. They had to hurry to get things done. He felt that there were not enough of the younger generation who were interested in things of historical importance. Occasionally he became impatient with the lack of interest: "I don't see why I keep bothering about such stuff. No one seems to care. If it was a 'prize fight' or a 'bridge party' or a 'movie stunt' or a 'testimonial to a war hero,' a whole crowd would be standing in line all night to 'reserve' places. . . ."

Yet, there was the almost unbelievable accumulation of correspondence imposed upon him by reason of the very prominence his historical work had won for him. Hardly a day passed without his receiving and answering letters of request. It will be of interest to note the way a few of the requests came:

". . . Will you kindly give me as much information as you have on 'The Draft Riots in New York City, July, 1863.' I am particularly anxious to present the Catholic side of the question in an acceptable manner, since the material will ultimately find its way to the screen. . . ."

". . . John Devereaux, born in Ireland in 1760 and died in Raleigh, N. C., is my great-great-grandfather. I wonder if you know who were the parents of John and Nicholas Devereaux of Utica and how these two families were related. . . ."

". . . Have you any personal details about Peter Blankinsop, the Baltimore publisher? I am making a note of the Catholic monthlies—his was the first, as you know, and, while there is ample information about his three distinguished children, all that relates to him seems to be that he married a relative of an Irish archbishop—quite sufficient of course for any reasonable researcher who cares when he was born and when he died. . . ."

And from one to whom he refers as an "Unfortunate victim of the Degree Mania."

"I appeal to your charity to help me in a difficult task. As I attend the summer session at . . . . and am working in the field of history, I have been given the thesis to write namely: 'The Attitude of the Catholic Press of New York Toward Organized Labor from 1840 to 1891'. . . ."

Thomas Meehan had written across this letter—"Imagine Organized Labor in New York in 1840! ! !"

Then a telegram:

"Please send me all articles and information on morals and social status of women today as compared with a generation ago."

"We are writing a history about (N.) and heard that there were accounts in the *Freeman's Journal* of the landing of 'six French nuns' in September 1840. Have you an account of their arrival? . . ."

". . . I am writing the life of my Grandfather, N. and have gotten pretty well along from his birth to the time when he was married. At present I am trying to show that a great deal of the trouble while he was a resident of . . . . was due to the fact that he was a Catholic. As far as I can make out when he first went to that part of New York State in 1823, there was but one Catholic Church and that was at Carthage 10 miles from his home. Is it possible to ascertain the name of the priest who was there then—1823 to 1830 say? The Catholic Encyclopedia say that there were but 5 Catholic Churches in New York State. Is that right?"

But not all of Thomas Meehan's mail was made up of questions. Occasionally his correspondents sent him fascinating items like the following:

"Another interesting item for me was the account of the Sacred Host that was brought by a Colonel from the Mexican battlefield. Reverend Father Edward Purcell, the Archbishop's brother, told us of the discovery by an Irish Catholic servant when she was dusting the books in the library. She very cautiously made inquiries as to how It got there and then told Father Edward. Evidently the priest who had the Blessed Sacrament was killed, and the soldier who found the Host kept it as a curiosity. The girl brought the book in which It was to Father Purcell and the Archbishop consumed It the following day."[44]

An examination of Thomas Meehan's own letters to friends and associates reveals interesting pieces of information like these:

"Dear old Father Anthony Cauvin was one of the most lovable and notable of the old timers. He came to New York in 1847 and after service at various mission stations he was made pastor of the Hoboken, N. J., section where he founded the Hoboken Church and that at West Hoboken, now the Passionist monastery. After ministering there until 1873 he resigned and returned to France where he died May 26, 1902. He came of an aristocratic family and two of his brothers were also priests. Napoleon III was one of his visitors in Hoboken and the church has a whole raft of gifts from him, Victor Emmanuel, etc. His sister was Duchess of Modena."

"The very first of these girls' clubs was started by Grace Dodge, daughter of the metal millionaire and a pioneer in the 'social service.' She began with some Irish girls working in the Higgins Carpet factory on the West Side. There were two to begin with. They brought in their companions to her home first. Then, as the number increased, she hired a house in West Sixth Street and organized a girls' club, the first ever in the United States and the model on which all the rest followed."

"I deposited the fifty bound volumes (from 1849) of my father's paper the *Irish American* in the Public Library, at the Forty-Second Street branch, after his death. He was one of Hughes' staunch friends and allies and there was not much put out by the Archbishop that is not printed in these files."

---

[44] Mother Garvey, R.S.C.J., Convent of the Sacred Heart, Torresdale, Pennsylvania, July 19, 1925.

AMERICA
NATIONAL CATHOLIC WEEKLY
329 WEST 108TH STREET, NEW YORK

EDITORIAL DEPARTMENT

Sept 19, 1941

Dear Doc:

It was a great sorrow not to be able to mingle with the elect at Wednesday's celebration and not to see you as I had anticipated, but I am glad to hear that you were in your old form, even if I fell down on the job.

This my 87th birthday, and if you had been in town you would had a ticket for a ringside seat at 200 Greene ave. Put in a reserve for the next, and in the meantime I am as ever your most devoted fan.

Thos. F. Meehan

TYPICAL LETTER OF THOMAS F. MEEHAN WRITTEN TO
MONSIGNOR GUILDAY OF THE CATHOLIC UNIVERSITY.
WASHINGTON, D. C.

"Dr. P. has another 'discovery.' He finds that in our Brooklyn foundation era there was 'only a sprinkling of Celtic Irish' before St. James was begun. 1 don't suppose he was ever in Brooklyn but if he'd spend a nickle for a subway ride the next time he visits Manhattan, and take a walk around old St. James' churchyard he'd find the tombstones advising him to take a few lessons in Hibernian patronymics."

The following excerpt shows another point of interest on which his advice was sought:

". . . I would like to discuss with you ways and means for starting a movement looking to the placing of Father De Smet in Statuary Hall, as the representative of one of the Western States in which he labored for the Indians."

Even while on his vacation, Thomas Meehan found interest in those things which another might probably not notice:

"Just now it is freezing here after a night spent under blankets and extra quilts. The ancient spinster named Gibbons who owns this house was charitable enough to leave all her domestic treasures at our service, so we can be comfortable. She is a Baptist, which sect is the only one that has not flourished in this section and the church, after a century of struggle, was sold for debt. She had the family pew taken out, and with a supply of cushions, it now serves as a comfortable lounge in the sitting room. The family Bible indicates a story: The Father, George Washington Gibbons, was born in St. Lawrence County, New York, in 1827, probably the son of an Irish Canal builder. The mother was Mary Cahill of Carismore, County Galway, Ireland (1833) and they were married in Trinity Church, New York City. It is easy to guess the missing links."[45]

Among the historical magazines to which Thomas Meehan contributed was the *Catholic Historical Review,* the official organ of the American Catholic Historical Society. A member of this Society for several years, he was elected a member of its Executive Council at a meeting held on December 8, 1928. In his letter of acceptance to Monsignor Guilday, he said: "Your letter was a very embarrassing surprise. I was never much of a 'jiner,' so now, when the dial points to 75 for the next stop, it is almost too late to begin even under the seductive influence of your nice

---

[45]Letter to Father Talbot, S.J., August 1927.

and appreciated compliment."[46] Others who were elected at this time were:

Right Reverend Thomas J. Shahan, D.D., Washington, D. C.
Right Reverend Arthur Connolly, Boston.
Carlton Hayes, New York, Professor of History, Columbia University.
Dr. James J. Walsh, New York.[47]

At the final meeting of the year 1939, on December 28th, Monsignor Peter Guilday proposed the following resolution which was unanimously adopted:

"At our foundation meeting in Cleveland (1919) Dr. John Franklin Jameson, then editor of the American Historical Review who made the inaugural address of the association was unanimously elected honorary member for life. Since his death in 1928 this place has not been filled and I propose to the Executive Council that this honor be conferred on Sir Thomas F. Meehan, K.S.G. Many splendid things might be said of Mr. Meehan, who is now in his eighty-sixth year. As the editor of the *Historical Records and Studies* and of the Monograph Series of the United States Catholic Historical Society of which he is now President, Mr. Meehan has not only given to American historical scholarship a treasury of data on Catholic life in this country but has also been the inspiration of many students during the last two generations."[48]

10. HONORS RECEIVED

Though Thomas Meehan shunned all publicity and was reluctant to receive any praise, his friends felt that his labors should not go unrewarded. Several times they prevailed upon him to accept the honor that was his due. Thus, at various intervals, he was the recipient of their good wishes. The United States Catholic Historical Society, the Brooklyn Alumni Association, and Fordham University were among those who welcomed the opportunity to demonstrate their regard and affection for him. The Most Reverend Thomas E. Molloy, Bishop of Brooklyn, expressed publicly, on several occasions, his great esteem for him.

---

[46]Letter to Monsignor Peter Guilday, January 12, 1929.

[47]*Catholic Historical Review,* p. 11, April 1929.

[48]Guilday—American Catholic Historical Association—*Catholic Historical Review,* p. 79, April 1940.

He was mentioned as a candidate for the Laetare Medal, one of the most notable distinctions that can be conferred upon a Catholic in the United States. Presented annually by the University of Notre Dame on Laetare Sunday, the fourth Sunday of Lent, this medal is comparable to the Golden Rose which is conferred by the Pope at Rome each year on some Catholic who has distinguished himself in world affairs.

Without his knowledge, the friends of Thomas Meehan sought to obtain this award for him. He would have been completely overwhelmed had he known that anyone ever considered him worthy of such an honor. The movements to make him the recipient received the endorsements of many of the hierarchy and outstanding members of the laity.

Cardinal Hayes wrote in a letter to Reverend Charles L. O'Donnell, C.S.C., President of the University of Notre Dame:

". . . I feel that I should not be doing my duty if I did not speak in the highest possible terms of Mr. Meehan and his unique and remarkable service in Catholic journalism as well as his writings in the history of the Church in this country. I venture to say that no one knows more, or has written much more than he on this very subject of the Church in the United States. He was trained in the life of the daily press of New York City and Philadelphia, an associate of John Gilmary Shea, Patrick Ford, Orestes Brownson, and other notable lights of a past Catholic era. . . ."[49]

Father O'Donnell's reply is full of cordiality:

". . . It is a signal honor Your Eminence does the University in recommending a candidate for the Laetare Medal. It is also another proof, among many proofs, of the interest Your Eminence takes in Notre Dame. As regards this particular candidate, Mr. Thomas F. Meehan, we have long known of his fine character and his scholarly achievement. None the less it is the greatest satisfaction to learn that Your Eminence so highly endorses his candidacy for the Laetare Medal."

Cardinal Mundelein, of Chicago, who as Auxiliary Bishop of Brooklyn had been pastor of Queen of All Saints Church of which parish Mr. Meehan was a member, favored the cause because he

---

[49]December 1, 1928.

considered him "worthy of any preferment for his long and efficient service in the cause of the Church."[50]

Right Reverend James A. Griffin, Bishop of Springfield; Most
Reverend Thomas E. Molloy, Bishop of Brooklyn; Monsignor
John L. Belford and Reverend F. X. Talbot, S.J., were enthusiastic supporters of this movement. Those of the laity who helped
to further the cause were: Percy King, President of the United
States Catholic Historical Society; Charles Ridder, of the *Catholic News;* Joseph Breen, Blanche Kelly, noted writer and one of
the editors of the *Catholic Encyclopedia;* Thomas Woodlock, the
1943 recipient of the Laetare Medal who said after receiving the
honor, "If anyone ever deserved this on all grounds, Thomas
Meehan did. It will always remind me of him."

Rita McGoldrick, Past Chairman of the Motion Picture Department of the Federation of Catholic Alumnae spoke for the
members of the Alumnae thus: "There is no record, no way to
trace the innumerable organizations, strong Catholic movements,
visioned undertakings that have been dreamed and planned and
encouraged by Mr. Meehan, for it has been his invariable way
to withdraw, so that others might win the high praise awarded
to success. In this particular Bureau of the International Federation of Catholic Alumnae, the success of the work has grown to
international proportions. Its cornerstone has been Mr. Meehan's
advice to us, his right judgments, his tireless efforts to win help-
ful contacts for us that our position with the motion picture industry might be strengthened. If this work has succeeded beyond
our dreams for it, then that success is due to Mr. Meehan's quiet
genius for helpfulness."

Although Thomas Meehan was not to have the honor of receiving the Laetare medal, which would have been a deserved reward
for his uncounted years of loyal, devoted and valuable services to
the Church in America, the nominating tributes are of themselves
proof of the high place he held among Catholic laymen.

However, his services did not go unrewarded; the future did
hold honors for Thomas Meehan. On February 25, 1931, he was
presented with a gold pen and pencil. The *Commonweal* tells us
that "It was an appropriate gift which the trustees of the United

---

[50]Chicago, December 31, 1928.

States Catholic Historical Society bestowed upon Mr. Thomas
F. Meehan at the testimonial banquet tendered to the editor of
the many invaluable publications issued by that veteran organization—a pencil and pen. The metal of which these tools of the
writers' craft were composed was gold. The symbolical, rather
than the material, value of that metal is what those who know
something about Mr. Meehan's work will think about. The highest of all literary values is the gold of truth. What American
writer has ever searched for it more assiduously, and found it
more abundantly, than Thomas F. Meehan in his fifty years of
service of the press? That the best years of Mr. Meehan's life
and the most useful fruits of his pen have been devoted to American church history, and to Catholic journalism of the most con-
structive and enduring kind, is acknowledged and appreciated by
those best qualified to know the inside facts of Catholic literature
in the United States. They are part and parcel of our native
Catholic tradition.

The future of Catholicism in this land has been made more
secure and more certain of worthy development, because of the
solid, enduring, patient character of the mass of historical research
and writing accomplished by Mr. Meehan. Perhaps nowhere else
in the world more than in the United States has there been a
graver danger of Catholics losing the memory of their own national
past, because of the almost irresistible pressure of more immediate and material cares and duties. And Catholics who cut themselves off from the past lose more than any other class in the
community, because the continuity of the Catholic tradition is
one of the most valuable assets of the Faith, both for those who
possess the Faith, and for society in general. Nobody has done
more to preserve the historical heritage of American Catholicity
than Thomas F. Meehan, and we hope that the golden pen and
pencil may maintain their invaluable labors for many years to
come."[51]

This presentation was followed in a short time by another honor.

It was in recognition of his sterling faith, his great services
and notable achievements as one of the outstanding Catholic laymen of this country that Thomas Meehan was named Knight of

---

[51]Commonweal, February 25, 1931.

St. Gregory by Pope Pius XI through the request of Most Reverend Thomas E. Molloy, Bishop of Brooklyn. Thomas Meehan considered as one of the happiest of his life, the day on which he received the following letter:

BISHOP'S HOUSE
367 Clermont Avenue
BROOKLYN, N. Y.

April 14, 1931

Mr. Thomas F. Meehan, K.S.G.
205 Greene Avenue
Brooklyn, New York
Dear Mr. Meehan:

It is my happy privilege to inform you that our Holy Father has graciously deigned to bestow on you the honor and dignity of the Knighthood of St. Gregory.

This gracious favor is accorded you by the Supreme Pontiff in recognition of your sterling faith and your notable services rendered to the Church especially in the field of Catholic journalism.

I shall arrange later for the formal presentation to you of the document of designation and the Insignia of Knighthood.

Please accept my most cordial congratulations and best wishes that you may long enjoy this well merited honorable recognition.

Sincerely yours,
✙ THOMAS E. MOLLOY
BISHOP OF BROOKLYN

The honor was conferred May 17, 1931, at Vesper Services in the Church of Saint Francis Xaxier, Brooklyn. Two other laymen were made members of the order at this time, Joseph Bradley Murray and John Tracey. The three laymen each in turn knelt before the Bishop as he placed upon them the red ribbon and the cross of the Order. Bishop Raymond Kearney, Chancellor of the Diocese and now its Auxiliary Bishop, read the Papal Bulls conferring the honor.

At this same ceremony, Monsignor David J. Hickey, Vicar General and the pastor of St. Francis Xavier's Church, a boyhood friend of Thomas Meehan, was invested with the insignia of Prothonotary Apostolic.

America voiced the sentiments of all the friends of Thomas Meehan in this editorial:

OUR FAITHFUL KNIGHT

That very prosaic term "servant" gives the real meaning, so the learned tell us, of "Knight," a word that recalls the age of Chivalry and bright romance. The Knight was the servant of the King but first of all, the servant of God and of Our Lady, bound to help all who were in distress. Some people in those days were in bondage to the Paynim, others were harassed by dragons, and not a few were held in captivity, according to the custom of the country, by robber barons or tyrranical kings. We strongly suspect that the dragon was merely a symbol for crime or ignorance, while Paynims did duty for infidelity, and kings and barons were the money lords of the time. However, that may be, the Knight was at the service of the weak, the ignorant, the oppressed and of all in need of succor.

This is but to preface the pleasure with which we learned last week that our Holy Father had made Thomas F. Meehan a Knight of St. Gregory the Great. The oldest and most beloved of *America's* staff, Mr. Meehan is the youngest in the brightness of his lovable spirit, and in his incorrigible optimism. His vivacity all but denies the undeniable fact that for more than half a century he has been a valiant knight in the service of the truth; and could we find it in our heart to hint a fault in Pius IX, Leo XIII, Pius X, or Benedict XV, it would be to express our wonder that this sign of recognition was not given him many years ago.

But the Pontiffs were not at fault. Unfortunately, our associate has not given due heed to the prohibition against hiding one's light continually under a bushel. Not having the fear of God before his eyes, he has on occasion strenuously denied that he had a light. Worse, we regret to say, in attributing to others projects which he himself began, sustained, and perfected, he has frequently fallen into that very rare crime which consists in bearing false witness against one's self. Not until this present year, was a Bishop of Rome able to discover this hardened sinner, and deal with him suitably.

The labors of Thomas F. Meehan in connection with the *Catholic Encyclopedia,* with the United States Catholic Historical Society and other historical societies, with *America* and other Catholic publications, have made all Catholics in this country his real if unconscious debtors. Of his services to the Editors, we cannot bring ourselves to speak, since any words at our command would grossly understate our admiration and our sincere gratitude. To everyone whom he has helped by his counsel, and to countless thousands who know this scholarly Catholic gentleman only in the works which he has inspired and fostered, but never claimed, he has been indeed a valiant knight, an untiring servant of the truth.

Before Thomas F. Meehan, their associate, the Editors who know so well his truly Catholic life, and who deeply prize the friendship given us and our predecessors these many years, stand at attention to salute. The pleasure which we feel in this mark of honor, bestowed by the highest authority on earth, is shared, we know, by our readers. May his years be as many, if that be possible, as the tale of his merits! May his mellowed wisdom long continue to instruct, and his gentle, courteous Catholic spirit, to edify and inspire us![52]

The secular press occasionally took opportunity to express public esteem for Thomas Meehan. John Heffernan of the *Brooklyn Daily Eagle* wrote:

In one of the older streets of Brooklyn dwells the most interesting octogenarian in the United States. Many years ago I had the privilege of association with Thomas F. Meehan, on the staff of Jim Bennett's *New York Herald*. Mr. Meehan, one of the prized members of the *Herald* editorial staff and correspondent in New York for several of the country's great newspapers, was then regarded by the wildest among us, and there were some wild spirits in our outfit, with profound respect. We considered him an exemplification of journalism at its best. An able writer, a stickler for accuracy and a gentle and generous comrade, the youngsters looked upon him as all they would like to be.

It was with great pleasure, therefore, that I read the following article in the Catholic periodical *America* a few days ago:

Thomas F. Meehan, K.S.G., was drafted for *America* from the *Catholic Encyclopedia* in 1909, and here he is still. At 85 he travels an hour's journey from Brooklyn every day, appears in the office with a genial smile, keeps us all informed about the current news, which he gathers from innumerable sources, superintends the proofs and toward the end of the day takes the subway and the street car back to Brooklyn. Suppression of any praise of himself is one of Mr. Meehan's traits. A week or two after the receipt of the following letter he casually mentioned it to us. Without his permission, though with his knowledge, we decided to share it with his *America*

---

[52]*America*, May 2, 1931.

friends on this occasion, since it was linked so closely with *America's* anniversary by his very distinguished friend:

Rome, March 10, 1939

Mr. Thomas F. Meehan, K.S.G.
New York City
Mr. dear Mr. Meehan:

The near approach of the 30th anniversary of the establishment of *America* affords me an occasion upon which to express to you my sincere appreciation of your long association with the members of our Society in their many literary endeavors, but most particuarly to convey to you my deep gratitude for your invaluable co-operation in the uninterrupted publication during 30 years of our national Catholic weekly. You helped in the compilation of the very first number and each subsequent issue has felt the touch of your hand.

You have shown yourself a veritable apostle of the press according to the heart of our late lamented Pontiff, consecrating yourself out of a spirit of genuine devotion to the Church in this field so rich in possibilities for good and for evil. Your work has been doubly appreciated by successive editors of *America,* not only because it was done with graciousness and exactitude but also because it gave evidence of scholarly research and richness of appropriate knowledge. Yet its greatest merit withal lies in this that so much of it was unseen of the world and unknown to men. Most certainly the Father who seeth in secret will in consequence be all the more generous in rewarding.

May Our Blessed Lord, to Whom you have dedicated your many years, bless all your days.

Very sincerely in Christ,
W. Ledochowski (signed)
General of the Society of Jesus.

It is impossible for me here to make a full record of the splendid work done by this fine gentleman of the old school, this example of what journalism was when its leading spirits considered their labor a high adventure worthy of the knightliest souls. I know he has written volumes about eminent Catholics in the United States; that his researches in the preparation of articles for the *Catholic Encyclopedia* were deep, and that recently he has prepared a valuable guidebook for Catholic points of interest in New York for the

World's Fair visitors. Well did he merit the congratulatory message from Ignatius Loyola's successor.[53]

The older generation knew Thomas Meehan personally; the younger generation knew him by reputation, and old and young united in paying him honor.

The Brooklyn Alumni Association which embraces in its membership many of the foremost Catholic professional, official and business men decided to present a medal yearly to some layman of the diocese whose distinctive character and service to his Church and fellow men merited signal recognition. At the annual dinner of the Association held at the St. George Hotel, on January 29, 1938, the first medal to be awarded was presented with approval of the Most Reverend Thomas E. Molloy to Thomas F. Meehan as a "tribute to his lifelong research and his extensive publications in the field of American history." Though he was prevented by illness from attending this dinner, a special telephone connection placed at his bedside enabled him to listen to the dinner proceedings and to the presentation of the medal which was received by his son-in-law Alfred B. Cadley.

Later, in the same year, on November 16, 1938, a special meeting of the United States Catholic Historical Society was held at the grand ballroom of the Center Club, Central Park South, to honor the editor of its publications. In recognition of his forty years membership in the Society and for his many years of devoted service as Editor of its publications, the Society presented him with a gold medal. Most Reverend Stephen J. Donahue was acting as honorary chairman of the Society, at the presentation.

After several preliminary remarks, President Percy J. King, K.S.G., who was presiding at this formal meeting said:

> "There are many formal distinctions of scholarship, intellectual activity, and Catholic culture that the name of Thomas F. Meehan recalls, when seen in a book or news publication, but there is another side of him, known to all his friends and many of his acquaintances, namely his delightful companionship, his ever ready willingness to share that vast store of facts, that reserve deposit of data, that a clear and unfailing memory has garnered in the eighty-four years he has bright-

---

[53]*Brooklyn Daily Eagle,* 1939.

ened the world with his presence. As Editor, and contributor to our publications, as inspiration and a model for us on which to pattern our conduct of the Society, he has proved a vital force in its last forty years. We have told him of our esteem and affection, at banquets and meetings, but words pass into the ether and no sound remains, we have presented him with written expressions of our admiration, but ink fades and parchment crumbles; so, this year, in recognition of his literary activities, his long membership in the United States Catholic Historical Society, and of his editorial work on our publications, we have decided to make in a more permanent fashion, an expression of our esteem, regard and admiration for him and his works, by presenting to him this gold medal, enduring in character, and true in its ring. It bears his portrait on its face and on the reverse side this inscription:

'Awarded for Distinguished Service to Thomas F. Meehan, K.S.G., Historian, Author, Dean of Editors, Born 1854, Member 1898. November 16, 1938.'

"Surely, Your Excellency, ladies and gentlemen, I know that you join with our Society in wishing him all the blessings that heaven can bestow on a good son of the Church who has fought as faithfully and as mightily with his pen as did the Crusaders with their swords; their battle was against men, his against error and falsehood. May Heaven spare him to us, with health of body and mind, to be the comfort and inspiration of our Society and Catholic Letters."

Heaven did spare him for just a few more years.

For years the members of the United States Catholic Historical Society had desired that Thomas Meehan accept the presidency of the Society, but he continually refused to do so. However, in 1939, they overruled him and he was chosen President of the Society to which he had given so much and to which he had proven such an inspiration. He was not able to attend the first meeting owing to slight indisposition. Reverend Francis X. Talbot, S.J., acted as Chairman in Mr. Meehan's absence and opened the meeting, at which Archbishop Spellman was present, and availed himself of the opportunity to emphasize the contribution of the absent President to the upbuilding of the Society. Father Talbot said:

"Mr. Meehan phoned me this afternoon, saying that a slight ailment kept him at home by the doctor's orders. It is unfortunate, because Mr. Meehan is one of the few living persons who can say that he knew every Archbishop of New York, and he wanted to be here this evening, Your Excellency, so that he might meet the new Archbishop of New York. May I make bold to say that it is your loss also, that Mr. Meehan is not here tonight, because he is a gentleman of the old school, whom all who know love, who is revered and respected, the dean of all historians of the United States."

To this, Archbishop Spellman replied:

"Since Mr. Meehan is not able to meet the Archbishop of New York, after having known the other five, if it won't be too much of a shock for him to see the falling quality of the Archbishop, I will be glad to call on him, and if I see that he is too disappointed I will say that the Archbishop is coming tomorrow. . . ."[54]

A few days later they met at the residence of the Archbishop in New York City.

Thomas F. Meehan was nearing his "four score and seven" when his Jesuit friends decided that it was their turn to show him that they appreciated his worth. This letter was sent to him:

FORDHAM UNIVERSITY
OFFICE OF THE PRESIDENT

April 30, 1941

Dear Mr. Meehan:

Having written so beautifully about the Fordham Centenary in *America* this year you will not be surprised to learn that we are fittingly celebrating the occasion with a solemn convocation. Among the many distinguished persons who will be recognized that day we are very anxious to have the only living alumnus of Governor Dongan's Jesuit School!

So at a meeting of the Board of Trustees last evening, it was voted unanimously that you be invited to accept the Honorary Degree of Doctor of Letters at the Centenary Celebration on September 17.

With kindest regards, I am

Yours very sincerely,

ROBERT I. GANNON, S.J. (signed)

The celebration was held on the day planned but because of ill health, Mr. Meehan was unable to attend. It was arranged, therefore, to postpone the presentation until a later date. It was

---

[54]*Records and Studies,* Volume XXX, p. 150.

THOMAS F. MEEHAN RECEIVING HONORARY DEGREE FROM FORDHAM UNIVERSITY

FATHER FISHER   THOMAS F. MEEHAN   FATHER TALBOT   FATHER GANNON

not until October 9th that Very Reverend Robert I. Gannon, S.J., Fordham's President, did confer the honorary degree of Doctor of Letters at a simple ceremony at 5:30 p.m. in the offices of *America*, the Catholic weekly review with which Mr. Meehan had been connected in an editorial capacity since 1909. Attending were: Reverend Francis X. Talbot, S.J., editor of *America*; the Reverend J. Harding Fisher, S.J., rector of Fordham University; and Thomas Woodlock, associate editor of the *Wall Street Journal*.[55]

The citation read as follows:

THE HONORABLE THOMAS FRANCIS MEEHAN

"To all who view these presents the Trustees of Fordham University and Fordham College give greeting in the Lord.

"This distinguished gentleman, Thomas Francis Meehan, now for sixty-eight years uninterruptedly has been engaged in the field of Catholic journalism. For the past thirty-two years he has assisted in the editorial work of *America* with the utmost devotion. No one is better acquainted than he with the Catholic history of New York, or for that matter of the Western hemisphere.

"Side by side this distinguished gentleman and Fordham University have traveled down the years. As a boy he set eyes on the Founder of the University, John Hughes, first archbishop of New York, and was a friend and even familiar of the succeeding archbishops, Fordham's patrons and protectors.

"Therefore Fordham University would consider herself wanting in duty to herself and this occasion if she did not unite with herself in the honors of this day this distinguished gentleman.

"Accordingly by these present we, the trustees of Fordham University and of Fordham College, authorized to that purpose by the supreme power of the State, bear witness that our dearly beloved, the Honorable Thomas Francis Meehan, has been advanced by us to the Honorary Degree of Doctor of Letters, and endowed with all the rights and privileges pertaining thereunto.

"And in proof thereof we have issued these present under the seal of our Corporation and the signature of the President of this College.

"Fordham University, New York, the seventeenth day of

---

[55] *Catholic News*, October 11, 1941.

September, in the year of Our Lord, nineteen hundred and forty-one."

This private ceremony of the presentation of the degree was one of the last functions attended by Mr. Meehan.

11. His Last Days

Though he had to slacken his journalistic work for a year or more before his death, Thomas Meehan continued to maintain an active contact with the *America* office and also with the United States Catholic Historical Society. His spirit was remarkable and he never lost interest in his work despite the fact that the lingering illness from which he suffered prevented his accomplishing all he wanted to do.

About two weeks before his death he wrote to Miss Herbermann, ". . . and I wish you would send me half a dozen envelopes and dittos of that slip that tells of the history of the Society and its accomplishments."

There was never any self pity or complaint because of the comparatively inactive life he was obliged to lead toward the end of his life. One was more apt to hear him joke about the lazy life he was leading. In a letter to Father Talbot he said:

> "Early today as I gazed out of the window at the delightful aspect, the weeping and wailing and gnashing of teeth began with extra vigor at the prospect that I could not get up even to vote. Then, the mail came in, and with it *America,* so the wailing paused, and, propped up with an extra bunch of pillows, the joy became unconfined as page after page unfolded the interesting contents. I kept thinking you must have been satisfied with the evidence it offered of the progress being made in the realization of your projected evolutionary results. . . ."[56]

at another time:

> "I am told to keep quiet, even temperature, stay in bed, you are improving, and meekly accept my fate while barking away in symphonic scaling. . . ."

and again:

> "Sorry I've been having a complete blackout of the ordi-

---

[56]November 4, 1941.

nary routine of a lifetime. But I suppose it is all in the run of the mill. If I didn't have a minute now and then over the phone with Dr. Henry Watts I wouldn't know I was alive. . . ."[57]

His end came peacefully on Tuesday evening, July 7, 1942, at the age of eighty-seven. He retained consciousness up until a few minutes before his death. He was not only conscious but vigorously alive. At nine o'clock he reminded his daughter of his medicine; shortly after that he fell quietly asleep.

The Mass of Requiem was celebrated in Queen of All Saints Church, Brooklyn, by the Reverend Francis X. Talbot, S.J. The Most Reverend Francis J. Spellman, Archbishop of New York, presided within the sanctuary and the Most Reverend Thomas E. Molloy, Bishop of Brooklyn, officiated at the last blessing assisted by Reverend Joseph Lamb and Reverend Charles Boyd, curates at Queen of All Saints Church, and Right Reverend Monsignor Edmund J. Reilly, administrator of St. James Pro-Cathedral.

Among the many priests in the sanctuary were the Right Reverend William E. Cashin of St. Andrew's Church, Manhattan; the Right Reverend Monsignor John C. York, late pastor of St. Brigid's Church, Brooklyn; the Right Reverend Joseph F. Conway, pastor of Queen of All Saints parish; Right Reverend Monsignor John I. Gorman; Right Reverend Monsignor John Jerome Reddy; the Very Reverend Robert I. Gannon, S.J., president of Fordham University; the Very Reverend J. Harding Fisher, S.J., rector of Fordham University; the Reverend John J. Wynne, S.J., the Reverend Gerald C. Treacy, S.J.; the Reverend John Toomey, S.J.; the Reverend Joseph A. Lennon, S.J., regent of School of Education, Fordham University; the Reverend Gerald Mears, S.J.; the Reverend Harold Gardiner, S.J.; and the Reverend John K. Sharp, pastor of St. Mary's Church, Manhasset, Long Island.

A formal expression of esteem and appreciation was sent to the family of Thomas F. Meehan in the following set of resolutions, drawn up by the Reverend Francis X. Talbot, S.J.

WHEREAS it pleased God, on the night of July 7, 1942,

---

[57] Letter to Father Talbot, S.J., January 2, 1942.

to terminate the mortal life of Thomas Francis Meehan, in the eighty-seventh year of his age, and to translate his precious soul into the new world of joy after the faithful reception of the Holy Sacraments, and

WHEREAS Thomas Francis Meehan from his earliest childhood until his last moments was exemplary in leading a true and thorough Catholic life in every respect, united kindliness with firmness and strength of character, was humble and unassuming in the spirit of Christ but also burning with the zeal of Christ, sought for little in material things but aspired to greatness in the spiritual sphere, always regarded his fellow men with understanding and charity, sympathizing with them and helping them in every way in his power, and had, therefore, won from all who knew him respect and love and veneration and had merited the close friendship of fellow-laymen, Religious, Priests, Bishops, Archbishops and Cardinals of the Catholic Church in the United States, as well as testimonials of affection and honor from His Holiness, Pope Pius XII, and from His Holiness, Pope Pius XI.

WHEREAS Thomas Francis Meehan had labored so zealously for the spread of the Kingdom of Christ through the Apostolate of the Press during sixty-seven years, and had most particularly devoted himself to the Apostolate of History, seeking to discover and spread the knowledge of the History of the Catholic Church in the United States, and

WHEREAS Thomas Francis Meehan, for forty-four years had been a member of the United States Catholic Historical Society, had known intimately the founders of this Society, was the Editor of the Society's publications, the *Historical Records and Studies* and the Monograph Series, and finally had been, since 1939, the President of the United States Catholic Historical Society. Therefore:

BE IT RESOLVED that the Officers and Members of the United States Catholic Historical Society record with sorrow their sense of loss in the death of Thomas Francis Meehan, their continued memories of him as one of the noble and saintly Catholic gentlemen of our times, and their determination to follow his ideals in the future guidance of the United States Catholic Historical Society, and

BE IT FURTHER RESOLVED that a copy of this Resolution be presented to his family, to his daughter, Katherine Meehan Cadley, his son-in-law, Alfred B. Cadley, and his grandson, Thomas Meehan Cadley.[58]

---

[58]Reverend Francis X. Talbot, S.J.

CHAPTER II

THOMAS FRANCIS MEEHAN AND THE UNITED STATES CATHOLIC HISTORICAL SOCIETY

REALIZING, with another devoted historiographer, John Gilmary Shea, that the future of historical research depended upon the preservation of extant documents, and the compilation of new works, Thomas Meehan made it his life's work to write and encourage others to write.

He found a willing co-laborer in Marc Vallette,[1] who had begun his writing career as the founder of the *Sodalist's Companion* at West Chester, Pa., and had organized the Long Island Catholic Historical Society, which was one of the "by-products" of the United States Catholic Historical Society. Like the latter organization, it had as its aim, "to collect all matters of an historical nature in relation to the Catholic Church, especially on Long Island." The scope of its work may be seen from the following program of its first public meeting, held on October 30, 1893, the fortieth anniversary of the consecration of the first Bishop of Brooklyn, at the Society hall on the corner of Clinton and Pierrepont Streets:

"Pre-Diocesan History of the Church on Long Island" by Marc Vallette, LL.D.
"Pioneer Laymen" by Thomas F. Meehan
"Pioneer Priests" by Rev. Michael G. Flannery
"The Diocese of Brooklyn" by Rev. James H. Mitchell, Chancellor of the Diocese.

Thomas Meehan was one of the trustees of the Long Island

---

[1]Marc Vallette, who was born in Basle, November 19, 1839, of French parents, came to the United States when very young. While a student he became interested in journalism and found employment in a printing office when he was fifteen years of age. In 1857 he founded the *Sodalist's Companion*, at West Chester, Pa. He developed aptitude as a writer and in 1867 became editor and manager of the *Philadelphia Catholic Standard* and in 1872 editor of the *Philadelphia Catholic Herald*. In 1874 he became assistant editor of the New York's *Freeman's Journal*. He subsequently succeeded John Gilmary Shea, with whom he had been associated in Catholic historical work in the editorial management of the *Catholic News*. In the course of time he became associated with Rev. White, D.D., as assistant editor of the *Brooklyn Catholic Historical Records*.

Catholic Historical Society, and George O'Hara was a co-founder.

On December 1, 1894, the Long Island Catholic Historical Society was incorporated under the name of the Brooklyn Catholic Historical Society.

The memorial to Peter Turner pioneer Catholic layman of Brooklyn was erected mainly through the efforts of the society; and later it inaugurated the movement which led to the founding of the Mitchell Memorial scholarship at the Catholic University in Washington.

Monthly meetings were held from time to time in the Chancery office. Papers on the earliest history of the Diocese were read. At one of the meetings Postmaster Furey of the United States Navy read a paper on "The Work of Madam Parmentier Bayer." A discussion was held at this meeting as to the wisdom of continuing as a separate unit since there were not enough interested people, especially among the Brooklynites. The majority favoring the historical work were from New York. Therefore, it was decided that instead of being a separate society, they should join the United States Catholic Historical Society which was then in its infancy.

It was in his association with the United States Catholic Historical Society that Thomas Meehan was able most effectively to achieve his aim—to write and to encourage others to do so.

Founded under the inspiration of the Third Plenary Council of Baltimore,[2] which recommended "the promotion of the preservation and study of the details and facts of our American Catholic history," the United States Catholic Historical Society saw the light of day on December 9, 1884, in the office of the Catholic Protectory of New York City at 415 Broome Street, when at the invitation of John Gilmary Shea and Doctor Richard Clarke, a

---

[2]The Third Plenary Council was called November 9-December 7, 1884, by Archbishop Gibbons. It appointed a Commission for the creation of a Catholic University. Elementary and high school education was discussed and a commission was appointed to prepare a catechism of Christian Doctrine. It also recommended the promotion of the preservation and study of the details and facts of our American Catholic history. John Gilmary Shea had been invited to this meeting and urged to write a history of Catholicism in the United States. The publication of this history was one of the important fruits of the council.

group of bishops met to discuss ways and means of spreading the knowledge of Catholic Church history. Among the most ardent supporters of the proposed foundation was the Rt. Rev. John Ireland, Bishop of St. Paul, who presided, and both Cardinal McCloskey and Archbishop Corrigan. A committee of three was appointed to draft a constitution, and a week later an organization meeting of the United States Catholic Historical Society was held in the parlor of the Xavier Union.[3] The first public meeting took place at the University Club Theater, 26th Street, New York City.

In spite of every plea, John Gilmary Shea declined the nomination for presidency. The choice, therefore fell upon Dr. Richard Clarke, a distinguished attorney, who was soon succeeded by Frederic Coudert, an authority on international law. The corresponding secretary was Marc Vallette.

Among other incorporators were several outstanding figures in Catholic life in New York: Monsignor McGean, Rector of Saint Peter's Church on Barclay Street; Patrick Farrelly, President of the American News Company, of which he was a co-founder; Dr. Thomas Addis Emmet, kin of the great Irish leader, and one of the most famous physicians of his time; Frank Churchill, publisher and lawyer; and Dr. Charles Herbermann, professor at City College and one of the editors of *The Catholic Encyclopedia.* Others were Cornelius O'Leary, Reverend R. L. Burtsell, and Charles Carroll Lee.

The guiding spirit of the new Society was, of course, John Gilmary Shea, whose curious middle name (Gil-mary: servant of Mary) bespeaks an ardent devotion to the cause of Mary and her Son. A native New Yorker, son of the principal of the grammar school at Old Columbia, John Gilmary Shea was one of the pioneer Catholic historians of the country. As editor of the *Catholic News,* from 1888 to 1892, literary adviser and editor of *Frank Leslie's Weekly,* and the author of numerous historical works, Shea was the first recipient of Notre Dame's coveted Laetare Medal. One of Shea's most valuable contributions to American Catholic Church history was the founding of the *Catholic Historical Magazine.*

---

[3]Xavier Union was an association composed chiefly of Catholic College gentlemen; this later became the Catholic Club of New York.

Records and Studies says of the infant organization:

"A society of this type was not one of great numbers, but for the enthusiastic few, the intelligent few who are filled with a desire of research, of doing all things to God's greater glory; those who feel they ought, after the example of the Apostles and prophets, under the guidance of the Holy Ghost to put into writing the wonderful accomplishments of Christian followers or encourage others to do so in order that generations to come might find in them the source of Divine light and Divine inspirations."[4]

The inactivity of the Society during 1885 and the greater part of 1886 proved that the Society's critic had spoken truly when he referred to the constitution as "breathing abundantly the spirit of zeal and ambition but lacking sobriety."[5] Convinced that their aim must be more modest, the members appointed a publishing committee with Dr. Shea as chairman. The first work of this committee was to propose the publishing of a quarterly magazine, and on January 1, 1887, the first issue of the *Catholic Historical Magazine* appeared.

Contributions from every part of the United States proved that, as the title of the Society indicates, it was not intended to be merely local in either membership or scope. That initial number revealed the vast historical learning of John Gilmary Shea, who in spite of failing health produced a series of articles in refutation of the claim that certain views of the Church's policy resulted in great numerical losses. Archbishop Corrigan and the prelates and priests assembled at St. Louis on the occasion of Bishop Kenrick's jubilee thanked him publicly for his service to the Church through this series, and later, when the Bishops and clergy in great numbers thronged the Cathedral in Baltimore to celebrate the one hundredth anniversary of the American episcopate, Archbishop Ryan of Philadelphia lauded Dr. Shea's great service to the cause of truth and the Catholic Church in America.

His end was heroic, recalling that of Venerable Bede, father of English historians, who by one last effort finished his Saxon version of the Gospels and then turned his face eastward to die.[6]

---

[4]*Records and Studies*, Volume XIII, pp. 174-5.
[5]*Records and Studies*, Volume XXIV, p. 13.
[6]*Records and Studies*, Volume XXV, pp. 13-14.

When John Gilmary Shea was told he was soon to die, he received the Last Sacraments, and then announced: "A single chapter of my book remains, and I must finish it." He called for his working materials, and with the damp of death already on his brow, wrote the last few words of the work he would not leave unfinished.

After the death of John Gilmary Shea the activities of the Society gradually declined, until 1898 when the work of reorganization was begun by Archbishop Corrigan and Patrick Farrelly, and a few zealous laymen. With the election of Dr. Charles Herbermann as an able and persistent President, activities were revived, and the quarterly magazine was succeeded by a formal volume of historical papers under the title of *Catholic Historical Records and Studies*, the first issue of which, in two parts, appeared in January, 1899.

The association of Thomas Meehan with the United States Catholic Historical Society begins with the inauguration of the new publication. A mutual interest in American Catholic History led Dr. Herbermann and Thomas Meehan to labor tirelessly to achieve the end for which the Society had been founded, the preservation of records and, subsequently, the interpretation in scholarly reports of facts significant in American Catholic Church History.

In the eighteen years during which Dr. Herbermann was President and editor of the Society, Thomas Meehan was always his willing and able assistant. When in 1905, Dr. Herbermann's sight began to fail, Thomas Meehan became an ideal collaborator, with whom to discuss editorial business, contributors, make-up and printing. His mind was a veritable storehouse where facts of Catholic history were piled up, digested and kept on file, and the team work between the two left nothing to be desired. When, therefore, upon the death of Doctor Herbermann, in August 1915, the Society looked for someone to succeed him as editor, it was not surprising that Thomas Meehan was asked to fill the vacancy.[7] As editor of *Historical Records and Studies* he maintained the high level of critical and historical verity that always marks the works of the Society, and soon became the living embodiment of

[7]Elizabeth Herbermann.

the organization—a treasury of Catholic historical knowledge and culture.

His labors were actuated by a desire to pass on to future genera-tions the true story of the Church in the United States, beginning with the experiences of missionaries whose records were often written in their own blood. They had no time to write their story, but it is handed down to us in the martyrology. Down through the centuries the written history of the Church has come to us and it is the duty of the chosen few to pass on to future generations the true story of the Church in her own land, the story of these early missionaries, their trials and hardships, their sufferings, and in many instances, their martyrdom. The fact that we live in a day of wonders should not make us close our eyes to all that has gone before. This was the spirit that actuated Thomas Meehan.

New York and Brooklyn life was ever the favorite milieu of Thomas Meehan's historical journeyings. His first contribution to the new publication of the United States Catholic Historical Society was an article on "The Draft Riots," (Volume I, part II), a subject on which he had first-hand information from his own youthful experience.

Through the exciting days of 1860-1861 when war and rumors of war filled the air, the voice of New York was for peace. On January 12, 1861, a Memorial signed by thousands of its citizens was sent to Congress, praying that the pending troubles might be settled by peaceful means. Later a mass meeting was held in Cooper Institute at which three delegates were appointed to con-fer with representatives of the six States that had already seceded, with a view to healing the breach by concession and compromise. At the same meeting, a Peace Society was formed with the vener-able Professor S. F. B. Morse, inventor of the telegraph as president.

Then came April 12, 1861. The old flag was fired on at Fort Sumter and fell dishonored before the palmetto standard. In a moment the current of popular feeling in New York changed. Self-interest withered. Patriotism revived and became uppermost. The air was electric with military ardor and patriotic enthusiasm. Regiments mustered in the armories or marched through the streets. On April 18, 1861, the gallant Sixth Massachusetts marched through the city on its way to the imperilled capital and added to the excitement. The gallant Seventh Regiment, the pride of New York, left on the 19th.[8]

The famous Irish Brigade which was later to become the famous Sixty-Ninth, First Regiment, a division of Meagher's Brigade was organized November 2, 1861. It left the city November 18. Archbishop Hughes and a group of Catholic and Civic leaders had assembled to cheer and encourage the troops. It was on this occasion that Thomas F. Meehan, then but a boy, made the acquaintance of Archbishop Hughes. Years later he playfully boasted of the fact that he was the only man living who had spoken to the six Archbishops of New York.

To the second volume (1900) Thomas Meehan contributed his first article on Elizabeth Seton, more commonly known as Mother Seton, daughter of an old New York family and founder of the Sisters of Charity at Emmitsburg. His interest in this fascinating story of Mother Seton is shown by the fact that he contributed articles on the same subject to the *Catholic World* (January 1910 —"One Hundred Fruitful Years") and to *Columbia* (August, 1922—"Paying Our Debt to Italy"). Again in Volume XXIX, *Records and Studies* carries "Tales of Old New York—Mother Seton's Residence."

Others in this series include:

(a) "The First Catholic Office Holder"; (b) "Grand Opera's Pioneer Patron"; (c) "A Catholic Literary Note on Poe's 'Raven'"; (d) "A Famous Landmark Passes"; (e) "A Day in Greenwich Village"; (f) "The New York Emmets"; (g) "Number Twenty-four Vesey Street," and "A Once Famous School."

Innumerable biographies appear throughout the series. His "In Memoriam: President Stephen Farrelly" is a notable tribute to a friend and associate of many years.

In Volume III Thomas Meehan appears as the chronicler of "Pioneer Days in Brooklyn." The personification of nearly a century of Catholic history, his life was almost contemporary with the Diocese of Brooklyn for the year it was founded was a year before he was born. He knew every detail of its early develop-

---

[8]"New York in the War of the Rebellion—1861-1865," compiled by Fred. Phisterer, Volume III, p. 2694.

men; he lived it; he loved it; he preserved it. Always eager to
lend himself to the service of others, he placed at the disposal of
the historical-minded of the Diocese all his own carefully cherished data about the early days.

Among the documents treasured by Thomas Meehan was a
letter from the Prefect of the Vatican acknowledging the receipt
of several volumes of *Records and Studies* which he had requested
through the columns of the *Catholic News.*

The letter reads:

Vatican City
July 29, 1938

THE UNITED STATES CATHOLIC HISTORICAL SOCIETY,
  NEW YORK
THOMAS F. MEEHAN, EDITOR OF THE
  SOCIETY'S PUBLICATIONS:

The Apostolic Vatican Library in my name wishes to express to you, sir, with greatest sentiments of gratitude, our
best and heartfelt thanks for the devoted and eager cooperation with which you have wished to favor it by your search
for the volumes missing here. Today, when we can admire in
its completeness our beautiful collection, we cannot, nor will
we ever forget the willing work of you, Illustrious Sir, to
whom we despatch cordial acknowledgment. We have in view
feelings of gratitude with which to turn distinction to all the
generous donors who were so responsive to our request, and
for those who have honored us with their revered names by
an inclosed card in the volume offered, we send our special
certificate of thanks separately. I enclose them in the present
letter and I ask you to send them to their destination.

With reverent feelings and deep regard I deign to sign
myself,

Devotedly always,
A. M. ALBAREDA, MC.[9]
(Prefect)

Whatever was of interest to the Church was also of great interest to Thomas Meehan. If he thought the cause needed publicity,
he saw that it reached the public in the best way possible. Nor
were his interests restricted to merely local matters. He realized
that one of the greatest problems in the United States is missionary progress among the colored. In order to present this to

---

[9] *Records and Studies,* Volume XXIX, p. 118.

the public he gathered the data that we find in his "Mission Work Among Colored Catholics."

When Holy Trinity Church in Williamsburg was celebrating its Diamond Jubilee, Thomas Meehan felt the occasion was an ideal one in which to relate the story of its pioneer missionary pastor, Father Johann Stephen Raffeiner. The account is printed in Volume IX of the *Records and Studies*.

The question of the status of the Church in a world seething with conflict was one that appealed especially to Thomas Meehan's truly Catholic mind. When President Roosevelt, in 1942, appointed Myron Taylor to be his personal representative at the Vatican, much criticism came from the mouths of non-Catholics fearing lest the Pope should move to the United States and try to rule the country. But they had forgotten that the First World War brought about a similar circumstance. Then it seemed that there was a probability that the Holy Father would find his rightful place as a sovereign in the general council of the nations. There was a demand that his diplomatic rights should be restored where they had been slighted, and that direct communication with the Vatican be re-established by those governments where for some years it had broken off. Direct diplomatic intercourse between the government of the United States is neither novel nor unprecedented. Mr. Meehan had traced this in his "Diplomatic Intercourse with the Pope."[10]

Volume XII was now being prepared for publication (1918). The world conflict at this time brought up many incidents that sent historians delving into records looking for facts to prove some statements that were being made. In 1918 a supposedly official statement[11] was made to the effect that at least 72% of the deserters of the Civil War were Irish. Mr. Meehan did not have that actual number at his command so he went to Washington to the War Department to investigate the statistics. He went through all the documents of the period but could not find information bearing on the point. The nearest thing he could locate was dated July 15, 1898, which said: "The whole number of

---

[10]*Records and Studies,* Volume XI, pp. 85-88.
[11]The document that went through the mails was entitled "Who Did the Deserting During the Civil War?"

soldiers of any given nationality in the service during the War
of the Rebellion is not known and it is impossible from any data
yet prepared to make even an approximately correct statement of
the number of percentage of deserters of any given nationality."[12]
Information is presented with Thomas Meehan's characteristic
accuracy and "historical-mindedness" in "Catholics in the War
with Mexico"[13] and "Catholic Activities in Our Two Great
Wars."[14]

Records and Studies are a veritable mine of historical erudi-
tion. In his own set of *Records and Studies* to which he had
added innumerable marginal notes and made many corrections,
there are various clippings neatly folded and placed between the
pages. He certainly had a system all his own. It is no wonder
that when anyone asked him for data on any subject he could
give full details, for he actually kept his *Records and Studies* up
to date, with his "pigeon-holed" references. As an example:
in Volume IV, there is a newspaper clipping from the *Sun,* June
30, 1937: "Miss Betty Morris wed to Harold Cochart," and on
it the notation in pencil "She is Dominick Lynch's great, great,
great granddaughter." These jottings and clippings would make
a volume in themselves. And what a volume that would be!

Under Thomas F. Meehan's energetic fruitful leadership the
Society published not only these studies, but also the Monograph
Series which are in the forefront of Catholic historical literature.
The first of this series is:

*The Voyages of Christopher Columbus: The Story of the Dis-
covery of America, As Told by the Discoverer.*

In 1892, the two hemispheres vied with each other to commemorate the four hundredth anniversary of the discovery of
America and to honor Columbus, the great discoverer. Church
and State did their utmost to enhance the impressiveness of the
celebration. The United States Catholic Historical Society, as a
Catholic, as well as an American and a historical association, decided to contribute its mite in honoring Columbus and his great
achievement. It presented to its members translations of the chief

---

[12]*Records and Studies*, Volume XIII, pp. 129-139.
[13]*Records and Studies*, Volume XII, pp. 39-65.
[14]*The Catholic World*, July 1918, Volume CVII, pp. 444-463.

writings of the great Admiral in which they found fresh and living the story of his deeds and his sufferings, of the feelings that stirred the undaunted heart which planned and endured so much. These journals were not written for the perusal of the public but for himself and his personal friends. They are genuine letters, more likely to emphasize the faults rather than the merits of the writer.

The documents included cover the main incidents in the life of Columbus from his first voyage of discovery to his death.

The translation of this work was done by Marc Vallette, in 1892.

The Unpublished Letters of Charles Carroll of Carrollton and of His Father Charles Carroll of Doughoregan, compiled and edited with a memoir by Thomas Meagher Field, was printed ten years after *The Voyages of Columbus.* The greater part of these documents were published for the first time—notably the letters which deal with the enactment and attempted execution of the Stamp Act and the excitement in the colonies consequent thereon.

Forty Years in the United States of America (1839-1885), by the Rev. Augustus J. Thebaud, S.J., the next in the series, appeared in 1904. Father Thebaud was an open-minded gentleman, interested in all the interests of the cultured man—science, art, politics, literature, commerce. The volume presents the judgments of a French Jesuit Father who instead of looking on the world from the inside observes it from the retirement of the cloister. It gives a general view of the country during those forty years.

He recounts his impressions, though not himself a witness, of the French Revolution and the Terror. The chapters afford a retrospect which shows how indelible was the impression made on the witnesses of those dreadful days and scenes and how deeply their recital of what they saw affected the generation which came after them. How strongly they haunted the memory of Father Thebaud is seen on every page of *Three Quarters of a Century* which appeared as monograph five.

In 1905, the Society presented *The Historical Sketch of St. Joseph's Provincial Seminary—Troy, New York,* to its members. It was prepared by Rt. Rev. Henry Gabriels, D.D., Bishop of Ogdensburg, whose biography by Charles Herbermann appears in the introduction. An account of early New York Seminaries is also given here.

This history was written at the request of many friends of the seminary who were anxious to preserve its memories and the deeds which would give glory to the Church. The author was the only one who was in full possession of the early history of Old St. Joseph's on Ida Hill in Troy.

Bishop Gabriels was born October 6, 1838, at the village of Wannegem-Lede in Belgium, and educated in the diocesan Seminary at Ghent, being ordained sub-deacon in 1860. In 1864 he was promoted to Licentiate of Theology and was thus declared worthy to be appointed to the Chair of Theology. Shortly before this time Archbishop Hughes had closed St. Joseph's Seminary in Fordham, having found it impossible to supply a competent staff of instructors. Several bishops planned a provincial seminary and the question of faculty members for the proposed institution arose. Their eyes turned toward Louvain, at that time the only Catholic University in Europe outside of Rome. Cardinal Sterkx, the Primate of Belgium, referred them to Bishop Delebecque of Ghent, who suggested the young Gabriels. After plans were completed, Rev. Henry Gabriels reached New York, October 17, 1864. He was welcomed by President Vandehende and Archbishop McCloskey, the successor of Archbishop Hughes, before sailing up the Hudson to their new home. No time was lost— the day after their arrival the new faculty began their work. As a teacher and lecturer, Father Gabriels was earnest, prudent, careful in his opinions and always conservative. The days at Troy, with their varied happenings, are told by him in this monograph which is the first one that Mr. Meehan edited. A further development of the Seminary topic is treated in *Saint Joseph's Seminary, Dunwoodie, New York* (1896-1921), by Right Reverend Arthur J. Scanlan, S.T.D. Not only the history of St. Joseph's is given here but also an account of the other seminaries of New York. Rev. Francis Duffy's *Seminary Life at Dunwoodie* is contained in this volume, published in 1922.

The fourth in the Monograph Series is *The Cosmographie Introductio*, by Martin Waldseemüller (in facsimile), followed by the *Four Voyages of Amerigo Vespucci*, with their translation into English, and also Waldseemüller's two world maps of 1507. One of these maps was a globe, the other a flat projection of the then known world. These two maps were the first that gave to the new world the name America. The Society printed this work in 1907 to commemorate the 400th anniversary of the naming of America. The attention of the learned societies of the world was drawn to the United States Catholic Historical Society by the publication of this valuable book.

Diary of a Visit to the United States of America is the fifth of the series.

Greatly as he marveled at all he saw in the Northwest during his trip in 1883, one cannot help thinking how much greater would be his amazement could Lord Russell return to make the same trip today. The Alaskan Highway is a marvel of the century. Lord Russell of Killowen visited this country in 1883. He was a man of such sound judgment, good taste, keen observation and Catholic sympathies that his views on what he saw in the United States could not fail to be instructive. We have a chance "to see ourselves as others see us" in *Diary of a Visit to the United States of America in 1883* by Charles Lord Russell of Killowen, Late Lord Chief Justice of England.

Two biographies find their places among these books: *The Life of John Baptist Mary David* (1761-1841), who was Bishop of Bardstown and founder of the Sisters of Charity of Nazareth. It was written by Sister Columba Fox of that Community.

The second biography (monograph XIV—1930) is *Gonzalo De Tapia* (1561-1594) founder of the first permanent Jesuit mission in North America. This magnificent treatise on the founding of the Jesuit Mission, written by Father W. Eugene Shiels, S.J., has been a great aid to students of early American Catholic History. It was written under the direction of Dr. Herbert Eugene Bolton, author of *Rim of Christendom,* the life story of Eusebio Kino.

The Catholic Church in Virginia (1815-1822), the story of the Catholic Church in Virginia during seven very stirring years, was written by the most eminent Catholic historian of today, Right Reverend Peter Guilday. The scholarly treatment of this accurate and thorough account makes this work one of the most valuable monographs in this series. In presenting this work to the Catholic Historical Society, Dr. Guilday has given a phase of Catholic history which had been gathered after a very careful research and presented mostly from the original sources. Interpretation has been mainly collateral.

Dr. Guilday became interested in history, as he himself says, "by accident", for his teacher, Father Heuser, had suggested it. He was sent to Louvain and for his doctoral dissertation wrote *The English Catholic Refugees on the Continent* (1559-1795), which was published in London as the first World War was breaking out in 1914. His researches for this historical thesis took him to all the leading archives and libraries of Europe, and it was the discovery of American boys and girls from Maryland and Pennsylvania in the English convents and colleges of the continent which had aroused his interest in American Catholic History.

He was appointed to the Catholic University and for 18 years enjoyed in his historical work the guidance of Bishop Shahan, an eminent historian of the first rank. He became managing editor of the *Catholic Historical Review,* which appeared for the first time in April 1915. He has been active in the American Catholic Historical Association, which was founded in 1919 for the purpose of creating a central organization for teachers and writers in the field of ecclesiastical history. Dr. Guilday's work in the field of American Church history is a monument to his untiring research and scholarly mind. The main purpose behind his great works is to rewrite with much new archival material the history of our church here from colonial times to the Secondary Plenary Council of Baltimore, in 1866. *The Life and Times of John Carroll* brings the history to 1815 and *The Church in Virginia* covered the period from 1815 to 1822. *The Life and Times of John England* carried the narratives from 1822 to 1842 and *The Life of John Hughes* which he is writing at the present time will cover from the 1842 period to the end of the War between the States.[15]

The rapidly growing library of *Records and Studies,* together with the Monograph Series, added a vast wealth of information to its great treasury of historical information on the publication of *Old St. Peter's* by Leo Ryan. It is a story of the "Mother Church of New York" written on the occasion of the one-hundred and fiftieth anniversary of the founding of the parish. It gives not only the history from its early days, with its warring trustee

---

[15]Guilday—*Book of Catholic Authors,* 2nd series, pp. 103-104 (Romig, 1943).

factions, through the Know-Nothing stage and the gradual change from simple parish life, to the new congregation of business people, but presents an account, worthy of reflection, on the historic significance of the edifice. Of this Church the late Monsignor Chidwick said: "This is a pioneer church that witnessed all the struggles of the pioneer days. Every cross that flashes in the morning light on the churches of this city and State speaks eloquently the reverence that must be paid to this old Church."[16]

In the *Quebec Act—A Primary Cause of the American Revolution,* Rev. Charles Metzger, S.J., shows how the people of the Thirteen English speaking colonies in North America reacted to those clauses of the Bill which guaranteed the Catholics of Quebec freedom to practise their religion. This volume gave to the series a valuable contribution on a topic which until its publication had not been discussed.

Since the general idea of the United States Catholic Historical Society is to collect all phases of historical material which will help to preserve the deeds of the missionaries, it was with great eagerness that Mr. Meehan received the account of the *Leopoldine Foundation in the United States* by Rev. Theodore Roemer, O.M.Cap. An account of its origin and functions appear in Monograph 13 together with the work done by *Pioneer German Catholics in the American Colonies* (1734-1784) prepared by Rev. Lambert Schrott, O.S.B., showed that the German Catholics played a prominent role in our Church history but little has been written of their deeds. Thus, while a complete history would require volumes, the Society welcomed even a shorter contribution to help keep alive some of the deeds of the German Catholics in America.

Thomas Meehan welcomed another contribution on missionary activities. After a thorough and comprehensive search through archival documents and records, the Very Rev. V. F. O'Daniel, O.P., in telling of the deeds of the *Dominicans in Early Florida,* presented to the students of American Catholic History an enlightening account of the work of the missionaries with the Indians.

Thomas Meehan had long desired to reproduce in facsimile the

---

[16]*New York Times,* November 24, 1930.

oldest book printed in North America, *Doctrina Breve*.[17] The United States Catholic Historical Society applied to the officials of the Hispanic Society for permission to do so. In a short time the following reply was received:

HISPANIC SOCIETY BUILDING
NEW YORK CITY

November 9, 1927

THOMAS F. MEEHAN, ESQUIRE

DEAR SIR:

We are sending under separate cover a photographic reproduction of the book *Doctrina Christiana* by Zumarraga. It is sent to you with the compliments of the President and the Trustees of the Hispanic Society of America.

Very truly yours,
THE HISPANIC SOCIETY OF AMERICA
Department of the Library

The *Doctrina Breve* was once the property of the Spanish premier, Don Conovas del Castillo, who gave it to the ill-fated Emperor Maximilian of Mexico, who was shot June 19, 1867. After that it was taken back to Europe, and sold at a Leipsig book auction, where a New York dealer purchased it and brought it back here. He sold it to Archer M. Huntington, who, in 1907, added it to the many attractions of the library of the Hispanic Society of America. Through the courtesy of Mr. Huntington and the Hispanic Society of America, the United States Catholic Historical Society restored it in facsimile to public circulation as a finely printed volume of 210 pages.

The title page of the book freely translated announces that the book is:

"A brief and very valuable compendium of the facts that pertain to the Catholic faith and our Christianity, in simple style, for the average intelligence. Compiled by the Most Reverend Sr. Don Fray Juan Zumarraga, first Bishop of Mexico and one of his Majesty's Council. Published in the said city of Mexico by his direction and at his expense in the year 1543."

---

[17]The first American Book was *Escalera Espiritual*—the spiritual ladder— by St. John Climacus, a Spanish translation, prepared in 1536 by Friar Juan de Estrade for the use of the Dominican novices of the Mexican Province of that order. No copy of this book, however, now exists.

It is, therefore, a Catechism or Manual of Christian Doctrine, the familiar text-book used also today for religious instruction.

In explanation of its origin and purpose, the Reverend Zephyrin Englehardt, O.F.M., has added a history of the book and of the other productions of the press Bishop Zumarraga set up as one of the adjuncts of his Apostolic mission in the City of Mexico. Father Zephyrin is well known for his long service in the world of letters, particularly for his monumental work on the "Missions and Missionaries of California."

This volume, *Doctrina Breve,* in facsimile, offers incontrovertible evidence, Father Zephyrin tells us, that the early missionaries of America were zealously active instructing the natives in what is worth while above all human knowledge, and that they availed themselves of the printing press as soon as it could be procured for the more rapid spread of the Gospel.

The last leaf in the book relates that the printing was completed on June 14, 1544. Hence, Columbus had set foot in the West Indies only fifty-two years when this *Doctrina Breve* left the press in Mexico. It was composed in Spanish and Indian by the first Bishop of Mexico City, the Right Reverend Juan Zumarraga, O.F.M.

The first English colony at Jamestown, Virginia, was not founded until sixty-nine years after the Aztec Indians had received the copies of the little book that told them in their own language whence they came and whither they were going, in short, all about their Creator and Heavenly Father.

Let the reader try to grasp the fact that, from the primitive hand press, in the so-called benighted Mexico, one hundred and sixteen different printed works were issued before England could establish itself anywhere in what is now the United States. Only fourteen out of the sixty-one years closing the sixteenth century could not boast of a single publication. Other years, however, made up for the omission by sending out from three to six new books a year.

Although works on Christian doctrine or catechisms and books of religious instruction held the first place as to the number of editions, there being twenty-five separate editions, not mere reprints, the subjects treated cover a wide field. Thus we find three works on theology; three on philosophy (including the Dialectics of Aristotle) ; seven on languages; six on medicine; two Lives of Saints; one history (Shagun's) ; two psalters; five rituals; four confessionarios; four sermons; four vocabularies or dictionaries; two song books; one psalmody with colored notes; one Missal; five on laws; one on nautical instruction; one arithmetic, etc.

Concerning the authorship of the various literary productions we find that the Franciscans are at the head with forty-one of the one hundred and eighteen books published in the sixteenth century. The Dominicans follow with seventeen publications.

They are closely pressed by the Augustinians who have sixteen to their credit. The Jesuits, who arrived in 1572, sponsored four books, and the Carmelites, following them in 1585, are the authors of one work, published in 1599.

So many literary works in almost every department of science and theology must have found readers, otherwise they would not have been written nor printed and reprinted. Such was the case. Moreover, the Mexican Indians, the Aztecs in the Valley of Mexico at all events, were gifted with a brighter intellect, and they were withal far more eager to learn than the natives in North America. The Franciscans noticed as much, and therefore, together with the first monastery rose the first public school in 1524, as Brother Pedro de Gante relates.

When more Friars had arrived, convents and schools were built in various localities. A part of the main building would be partitioned off for the boys. Oftentimes there were as many as 600 and 800 boys housed and fed by the missionaries.

At stated hours the missionaries exercised the children before an altar in the prayers and the ceremonies of the Church, and thus instilled into the hearts of their pupils love for the divine worship. The Fathers also taught the boys to read, write and sing, and with a success which exceeded the most sanguine expectations.

It was more difficult to bring religious and secular knowledge to the girls, because the Indians would not permit men to approach the female sex. Emperor Charles V, hearing of the lack of means to attract the Indian women and girls, ordered a convent to be built for the Poor Clares, who were to teach the daughters of Indian as well as Spanish parents. A number of Sisters of the Third Order Regular accompanied the Poor Clares from Salamanaca under the personal care of the wife of Cortes in 1530.

As early as 1525, however, several ladies had already sought shelter from the world in a house set apart for them by Ferdinand de Sylva, Count of Centifonto. Here they accepted and professed the Rule of the Third Order of St. Francis. This may, therefore, be regarded as the first convent of women in the New World. It was situated in the City of Mexico. The same pious nobleman erected an academy for young ladies, who were to be educated by the Sisters. Schools and academies for girls thereafter rose in various parts of Mexico under the Rule of the Third Order of St. Francis.

Here we have the answer to the question why so many books were printed even in the very first century of the Christian history of Mexico. The attentive readers will also have learned that the first schools in America were opened in Mexico under the banner of the cross about a century before the Puritans landed in New England.

This reproduction of America's oldest book by the United States Catholic Historical Society was therefore a very notable accomplisment and it makes a historic literary relic.[18]

A copy of this volume was given to His Holiness Pope Pius XI at a private audience on June 9, 1928. The committee who went to Rome were Miss Elizabeth P. Herbermann, the Executive Secretary of the Society; her sister, Miss Louise Herbermann, and Miss Cornelia C. Craigie. His Eminence, Cardinal Hayes, the official head of the Society, gave them a formal letter of introduction, and the Very Rev. Monsignor Joseph A. Breslin, Vice-Rector of the American College, presented them to the Holy Father.

The Book was bound in white leather, hand tooled in gold and lined with white moire silk. When he looked at the facsimile reproduction of the old black letter type of 1544, his well-known love of books was manifested by repeated exclamations of pleasure as he scanned and turned the leaves of the volume.

It pleased Thomas Meehan whenever any of the Society's Volumes were being appreciated and sought after by librarians and students of historical research both here and abroad. The valuable records and data contained in the volumes of the Monograph

---

[18]*Catholic News*, May 12, 1928, by Thomas F. Meehan.

series and all the numbers of *Historical Records and Studies* have time and again proved of special service to writers on the progress of the Catholic element in the evolution of this Republic.

Among those asking for copies of the publications was the Rt. Rev. Monsignor Eugenio Tisserant, Pro-Prefect of the Vatican Library, from whom the following communication, as translated from the Italian original was received:

Vatican City,
August 27, 1932

UNITED STATES CATHOLIC HISTORICAL SOCIETY
NEW YORK, N. Y.

There has arrived at this Apostolic Library, Volume I, Part I of the *Historical Records and Studies* series, sent through the special courtesy of your notable Society, in order that we may complete our collection.

I feel bound to express my grateful feelings for the solicitude and interest shown toward this Library, and I especially wish to thank you in advance for any missing numbers of your periodical which you may be able to procure for us.

Please accept, with my high esteem, my very best wishes.[19]

(signed) EUGENIO TISSERANT,
Pro-Prefect

Monsignor Tisserant is one of the most distinguished officials of the Vatican Curia. He has traveled extensively and is widely known for his scholarship in oriental studies.

At the age of twenty-four he was brought to Rome by Pius X as an expert for the Biblical Commission and to act as curator of oriental manuscripts in the Vatican Library. At the invitation of the Carnegie Trustees he came to the United States to study cataloguing methods. In 1928, he went to Oxford as a Pontifical delegate. He became Librarian at the Vatican when Monsignor Mercati retired.[20]

The publications are now also to be found on the shelves of the world-famous Bodleian Library of Oxford University, in connection with which is an interesting incident. One of the members of the United States Catholic Historical Society, the Rev. Dr. Joseph F. Thorning, S.J., chairman of the Committee on Relations of the United States and Europe of the Catholic Association for International Peace, in the course of a year in Europe making

---

[19]*Records and Studies,* Volume XXII, p. 279.
[20]*Records and Studies,* Volume XXII, p. 279.

a survey of the world's social and economic problems, visited London, Paris, Berlin, Vienna and Rome and was a delegate at the Conference at Geneva and Lausanne and kept constantly in touch with the members of the American delegation at Geneva. During his tour he had a special interview with Ramsay Mac-Donald, Andre Tardieu, Dr. Breuning, Count Apponyi, Lord Robert Cecil, Mussolini and a private audience with the Holy Father. The notable feature of these incidents he has outlined in a series of very interesting letters to *America* for which review he acted as special correspondent.

While in England he visited the great Bodleian catalogue at Oxford, where he saw exhibited on one of the shelves a copy of the very famous *Bay State Psalm Book,* printed in January, 1639, at Cambridge, Massachusetts, and styled in the Bodleian catalogue as "the earliest American book."

Dr. Thorning called the attention of the Bodleian librarian to this and told him it was an error, because the oldest American book was the *Doctrina Breve* published in June, 1544, at the City of Mexico, by the direction and at the expense of Bishop Zumarraga of that See, and the only perfect copy of which was included in the collection of the Hispanic Society in New York. This oldest American book, he added, was reproduced in facsimile in April, 1928, by the United States Catholic Historical Society of which he was a member.

The Bodleian librarian was much interested and surprised, as he had never heard of the *Doctrina Breve*. Dr. Thorning assured him that as soon as he got back to New York he would see that a copy of the facsimile of *Doctrina Breve* be sent with the compliments of the United States Catholic Historical Society to the Bodleian Library. This was done immediately by the editor, as Dr. Thorning promised, and the Bodleian Librarian sent this acceptance in reply:

Bodleian Library
Oxford, 20 August, 1932.

DEAR SIR:
I beg you to accept my sincere thanks for the undermentioned work which you have graciously presented to the Library of the University.

I am yours faithfully,
E. LOWE (signed)
Acting Librarian

The *Doctrina Breve* in facsimile edited by yourself, 1928, Thomas F. Meehan, Esquire.[21]

A phase of journalism that had a special appeal for Thomas F. Meehan was early Catholic newspapers and magazines. He made an intense study of the early Catholic periodical literature of the United States tracing its origin, scope, development, progress, design, and policy. He was always poring over files of these pioneer journals in quest of any morsel of information dealing with the different phases of history. He did not limit his search but sought especially to trace the effect they had upon the lives of the readers. The whole disposition of Catholic journalism during the early decades seems to have been to promote harmony by removing from the pathway of Protestants the groundless prejudices and prepossessions which had grown into social barriers due chiefly to the circulation of misrepresentations and calumnies by enemies of Catholicism in Europe and America and to the supineness of the Catholic body in the face of such gross fabrications.[22]

Early attempts at building up a Catholic press were the objects of Thomas Meehan's painstaking research. In *New York's First Catholic Newspaper,* he tells in an interesting manner the early days of journalism in America, speaking principally about Thomas Lloyd, an almost forgotten pioneer in the field of journalism. Lloyd was credited with being the founder of American shorthand writing and the official reporter of the early sessions of Congress. It is claimed that when Washington stood on the balcony of Old Federal Hall in Wall Street, New York, to take the oath of office as first President of the United States and to deliver his inaugural address, it was Lloyd who stood beside him and reported it. This report was laid before Congress on the following day and a copy of it given to the Gazette of the United States which printed it on May 21, 1789.[23]

But, New York's distinctively first Catholic newspaper did not appear until 1825. It was the *Truth Teller* and its first issue was dated April 2, 1825. There was no mention of anything Catholic in its first five issues. The paper continued for many years until

---

[21]*Records and Studies*, Volume XXII, pp. 279-281.

[22]Foik—*Pioneer Catholic Journalism*, p. 9.

[23]Martin I. J. Griffin in the *Philadelphia Catholic Standard and Times,* September 21, 1902.

it was bought in 1855 by Patrick Lynch and William Cole, publishers of the *Irish American*. They published it for a short time separately and then merged it in the *Irish American*. It was with this newspaper that Thomas F. Meehan launched on his journalistic career, after his graduation from St. Francis Xavier College.

The newspapers of the period around 1840 seem to give a contemporary view of the rise and spread of Catholicism in America. It was with great satisfaction then, that when this all important phase in the development of our national unity was so carefully studied and presented by Dr. Paul J. Foik, C.S.C., Thomas Meehan edited it for the Society. "Pioneer Catholic Journalism" traces the history of this literature from *The Michigan Essay*, considered the pioneer of all Catholic journals since it owes its beginnings to the Rev. Gabriel Richard, one of the early missionary priests of the Northwest, to the *Freeman's Journal*, which suspended publication in July, 1918.

Parallel to this study of journalism in the early days of the nineteenth century was the consideration of the literary trends during the same period. "Catholic Literary New York" (1800-1840), was written by Thomas Meehan for the *Catholic Historical Review* (January 1919). He developed this much further in "The Centenary of American Catholic Fiction," during 1929, the hundredth anniversary of the first Catholic novel, *Father Rowland* by Dr. Constantine Pise.[24] This was a story with a purpose which it aptly served, and that was to offset the calumnies of a vicious anti-Catholic book, *Father Clement,* one of the outcroppings of the then rising storm of "native Americanism."[25]

---

[24]Dr. Pise contributed much in the literary field. He was ordained a priest on March 19, 1825, and after his ordination was attached to the Baltimore Cathedral for several years and then was transferred to St. Patrick's Church in Washington. Society at the capital lionized him and on the motion of Henry Clay, he was appointed Chaplain of the United States Senate on December 11, 1832, which office he held for two years. He then went to Rome and appeared at the Sapienza for public examination for the degree of Doctor of Divinity. Pope Gregory XVI personally bestowed on him the doctor's cap and ring and in addition made him a Knight of the Holy Roman Empire. On his return to the United States in 1834 he accepted the invitation of Bishop Dubois to become associated with the Diocese of New York. In 1849 Bishop Hughes sent him to Brooklyn to found the new parish of St. Charles Borromeo.

[25]*Records and Studies*, Volume XIX, p. 52.

A work in this literary field which had been of great interest to Thomas Meehan for many years was the reproduction of the first American novel. He had made some preliminary arrangements for this, but did not live to see its completion. The work was carried on by Reverend Dr. Thomas J. McMahon, his successor as editor of the Society's publications in the publication in facsimile of *Adventures of Alonzo* by Thomas Atwood Digges (1741-1821), a Catholic and a native of Maryland. In planning this volume, Mr. Meehan wrote:

"According to Philip Brooks, editor of 'Rare Books,' *New York Times Book Review* (Sept. 14, 1941), Robert H. Elias of the University of Pennsylvania has compiled conclusive evidence that the first American novel published anywhere and written by a native of the United States, was *Adventures of Alonzo: Containing Some Striking Anecdotes of the Present Prime Minister of Portugal;* published in London 1775 by Thomas Atwood Digges of Warburton, Maryland. . . . That the name of a Catholic should 'lead all the rest' of American novelists is a find that ought to set research students in a very busy mood.

"The author was a member of one of the pioneer Catholic families of the Maryland Calvert colony. William, John and Charles Digges were among the insurgents led by the Carrolls, who threatened a mass emigration in 1728 in protest against the penal laws and intolerance on the Protestant ascendancy that controlled affairs. Fathers John and Thomas Digges were Jesuit missionaries active 'in the counties' for most of the concluding years of the last century."

The publication of this volume brought to a close a series of Monographs and Studies that will always be a lasting monument to Thomas F. Meehan, whose life was so devotedly spent in the cause of American Catholic history.

CHAPTER III

THOMAS F. MEEHAN AND AMERICA

(This chapter is the work of the Reverend Francis X. Talbot, S.J., Editor-in-Chief of America and for twenty years an intimate friend and associate of Thomas F. Meehan.)

AT THE age of fifty-five, Thomas F. Meehan entered upon a new and long career. Through thirty-five years previously, and ever since his graduation from St. Francis Xavier's College, New York, he had been variously engaged in journalism, as Managing Editor of *The Irish American,* as a reporter and correspondent for secular newspapers, and as a contributor to many periodicals. Then in 1909, he joined the staff of the National Catholic Review of the Week, *America.* Thereafter, his association as editorial assistant continued through thirty-three years, until his death on July 7, 1942.

Elsewhere in this Memoir, it is related that Mr. Meehan was secured, in 1905, by Reverend John J. Wynne, S.J., as Manager of the Editorial Room of the *Catholic Encyclopedia.* About 1908, Father Wynne was actuating the establishment of a new weekly that would be for American Catholics what the *Tablet* of London was for England and the English-speaking world. Early in 1909, the plans for the publication of *America* had fructified. Father Wynne, as the founder and the first editor, drafted Mr. Meehan from the *Catholic Encyclopedia* and placed him in charge of the editorial production of the first issue of *America.* He continued to supervise all the succeeding issues until a few years before he died.

In 1941 and 1942, an effort was made to gather the personal recollections of those associated with *America* during its earlier years. Mr. Meehan was enthusiastically interested in this project. He was fertile with ideas as to those who could tell the story of the first days and earlier decades. He loved to relate innumerable anecdotes about *America* and its editors. But he would never write them out, so that we might preserve them for the history. Some day, he would promise, he would sit down and "tell all he knew."

He did, however, begin to fulfil his promise in regard to

America. In the morning mail of July 7, I received a bulky envelope addressed in his own square handwriting. The manuscript recalled some of his early memories. In the evening of the same day, I received a telephone call that he was sinking rapidly. Shortly before ten that night, Mr. Meehan passed quietly to God.

The covering letter with the manuscript was gay and alert, as usual. It is so illustrative of him, even up to the last day, that it can well be placed in evidence. Mr. Meehan wrote:

July 6, 1942

DEAR F. X. T.

Here's Chapter I for your Archives, and therefore you cannot say I failed you in your hour of need. I did it over half a dozen times to try and get it into satisfactory shape, and I still don't like it. It was trailing into a J. J. W. memoir, so I cut all that out. That book he got out about the "Academy" ought to be in the Archives. A copy must have come to the office.

This week's *America* is a fine, up-to-date paper. Interest and satisfaction in every department.

T. F. M.

On the other side of the sheet, he added a note that was characteristic of his awareness and devotion. He must have chuckled as he wrote it:

"We have heard that the wedding was a great success. But one of your friends, who had not seen you for some time, was shocked at your 'venerable' appearance. It seems as if this ought to be reported to the F.B.I. for immediate executive action."

The manuscript itself was dated July 1. It consists of nineteen handwritten pages. Every letter is clear and firm, and the corrections are very few. The titles were written out, with the caps indicated. Mr. Meehan's last writing follows:

AMERICA
CATHOLIC REVIEW OF THE WEEK
NEW YORK

VOL. 1, No. 1　　　APRIL 17, 1909—TEN CENTS

As March, 1909, was ending, I was pushing along the proofs for publication of Volume V of the Catholic Encyclopedia, of which, for the previous three years, I had been

July 6-1942

Here's Chapter I for the archives and therefore you can not say I failed you in your hour of need. I did it over half a dozen times today and got into satisfactory shape and I still don't like it. It was trailing into a J.J.W. memoir so I cut all that out. That book he got out about the "Academy" ought the in the archives. A copy must have come to the Office.

This week's America is a fine up to Date paper. Interest and satisfaction in every department.

T.F.M.

THOMAS F. MEEHAN'S LAST LETTER, WRITTEN TO FATHER
TALBOT, OF *AMERICA,* ON THE DAY BEFORE HE DIED

the production Managing Editor. I received a letter from
the Reverend John J. Wynne, S.J., in which he said his long-
cherished ambition to be the founder and Editor of a Catholic
weekly was about to be accomplished, that the *Messenger*
magazine was to stop publication and a weekly review would
be issued in its place, of which he would be the Editor.

He had rented and furnished the Alsop mansion in West
Washington Square and Washington Place for the office of
the publication, the date for which had been set for early in
April; and the Associate Editors, appointed from the various
Provinces, were already there preparing the material for the
first issue. He wished me to leave the Encyclopedia and join
the staff of the new periodical. He also thought there should
be another taken from the Encyclopedia staff, and that I
should choose either James C. Gray (now, 1942, Literary
Editor of the New York *Sun,* died in November, 1943) or
Thomas Haggerty (now Editor of the Wagner Publications).
My selection was Gray, knowing his broad culture, experience and familiarity with French and Italian. I suggested that
Gray should go to the new office at once.

For myself, in order to avoid delay and confusion, I thought
I should remain with the Encyclopedia until I had finished
sending the last forms of Volume V to the printer. To this
Father Wynne agreed. So I got out the volume and departed
the second week in April to work on the new venture. Looking back, it seems strange that, although I had heard of it,
the details were somewhat of a surprise, probably because of
the time they took to perfect; our personal contact has not
been constant.

I remember when the project of a paper had been first
mentioned, the question of the name came up. I suggested
that, to carry out a continuity and sequence, the *Truth Teller,*
New York's first Catholic weekly—the founder and owner of
which was George Pardow, father of a pioneer New York
priest and grandfather of two notable New York Jesuits—
should be revived in a new series. As my grandfather, Patrick
Lynch, was its last owner—having brought it in its moribund
days from the surviving owner, William Denman, and suppressed it in 1855—the title was a sort of family asset. I
offered to have it formally transferred to the new outfit, and
thus complete the chain. Father Wynne thought it an interesting idea, but did not adopt it. The name *America* was
taken, suggested, I understand at the time, by Father Thomas
Gannon, S.J.

When I got downtown I found Gray busy with the foreign
papers, making notes of interest, and the Editorial Staff put-

ting together the material for the contents of the first number. The Alsop house, at the corner of Washington Place and West Washington Square, was a fine five-story structure with an extension covering the back of the lot. It was the city residence of the English brewing company, their country villa being at Newton, Long Island—115 acres of land—which Archbishop Hughes bought in October, 1845, and made into the first section of Calvary Cemetery. The house was splendidly built, all the wood trim being mahogany and rosewood, with silver doorknobs and escutcheons. General George B. McClellan, of Civil War fame, had been its tenant while he was Public Works Commissioner, building the New York dock system; and Mrs. Hicks-Lord, social leader, was a later occupant.

The street floor was used as the business office, store-room, kitchen, etc. A large salon, next the main entrance, made an attractive reception-room; and other rooms, back along the extension, were arranged for a neat Chapel, dining-room and assembly-room. Upstairs were the bedrooms for the Editors.

The Community started with this membership:

Reverend John J. Wynne—Editor-in-Chief

Associates: Reverends Michael O'Connor and F. S. Betten, St. Louis; Michael Kenny, New Orleans; D. Jacobi, Cal.; Louis H. Drummond, Canada; E. P. Spillane, New York.

Later Joseph Williams was made Minister and Business Manager.

Externs: Thomas F. Meehan, James C. Gray: copy reading, translations, exchanges, printers' contracts, pressroom-publication details, general utilities. J. M. O'Rourke: advertising and circulation; Frank Meany, Inc., printer and press work.

The Editors kept preparing copy and having it set up, and proofs shown and read. Then, when they had decided definitely on the contents, the various departments of the paper and the order in which they were to be used, I was given a set of proofs, the layout of the contents, and told to go ahead and make up Number I, Volume I. I think it was on the afternoon of Tuesday, April 4. This was not a hard job. There was no dummy, and all that was necessary was to stand over the stone-man and see that he lifted the matter from the galleys into the page form in proper order—an easy task, as there were no spread-heads and complex features.

The pages were sent to the Editors, and then the trouble began. The Editors had had no technical experience in writing copy for the printer, in the necessity for conforming to style, and the disastrous results of changes in the text. In this last contingent, the Editor-in-Chief was the most conspicuous offender. In this, as in his previous editorial efforts, he disdained traditional typographical rules, and edited his copy in the proofs. He cut, inserted new lines, transferred, without any regard for the consequences. The "corrected" pages came back two, and sometimes three times, and we spent the afternoon and evening making up and remaking the page-proofs—an indefensible waste of energy and time. It was two o'clock the following morning when we had the final page-proofs in accord with the Editor's marks. We took the bundle over to Washington Square, but of course the house was dark and had been shut up for several hours, so we shoved the proofs into the mail-box slot in the door and went home to bed ourselves.

Later in the day I came back and was given the revised proofs for the printer to make up the forms, "two-sixteens," of the issue. This was done, and they were sent to the presses and a dozen sheets run off, and given to the Editors for the final revision which did not make any further delay—and *America,* Volume I, Number 1, was an accomplished journalistic fact. The delay and confusion of the make-up could hardly be excused, but an extenuation was offered that, as it was the first copy of so important an offering to the public by the Society, the greatest care had to be exercised that it contained no blemish of any character.

To the intense joy and satisfaction of all immediately concerned, the reception of the new national Catholic Review of the Week was most favorable. Congratulations and approval came from all over the country, and from the most distinguished and authoritative personages—clerics and laymen. It was looked on as promising to rank immediately among the foremost exponents of Catholic thought in the English-speaking world.

In October, it was found that Gray was not needed for the office work, so he went back to the Encyclopedia. With the succeeding issues, the Editors gained typographical experience and things ran along smoothly, but it developed that Fathers Betten and Jacobi had fulfilled their assignments, and so they returned to their Provinces. Fathers James J. Daly, St. Louis; and Henry Woods, California—two splendid acquisitions—took their places.

The Editor, with his wonted super-energy, was busy with plans and projects. The city needed a new courthouse for its tribunals, so it was reported that a site on University Place, facing Washington Square, had been selected. With that in view, he persuaded the Fordham officials to buy, with the idea of making it its Law School, the house next to the *America* office, and he rented it as an *America* annex. Entrances were broken through the walls on the various floors, and some of the Fathers who did not have comfortable quarters in the small rooms on the top floors of the Alsop house moved over. The large room on the parlor floor at the entrance he designed to be a sort of *America* information bureau, where patrons and strangers could call and register, have their mail addressed and kept for them, and all possible attention given to their convenience and comfort. He put a desk in there, with one of the office staff to carry out the welcoming program; but it never got any further than that.

There were other plans and projects flitting through the ever-active brain of the Editor, and if they did not meet with approval of the staff there was no outward manifestation of dissent. I knew there were differences in regard to policy, but that was none of my business. I enjoyed the most harmonious relations with all the staff. The Editor knew I understood just how he wanted the details carried out, and so I conformed; therefore I saw that the mechanical routine was lacking in no way. Then came the climax.

The issue for April 9, 1910, had been sent out, and, as I came to the office one morning of that week, Father Spillane met me in tears. Something dreadful had happened. A cable from Rome had removed Father Wynne as Editor, and Father O'Connor was in charge, *pro tem*. Of course it was a great shock. The dual editorship of *America* and the Encyclopedia was too much of a burden, for Father Wynne, so it was announced that he was withdrawing from *America* and hereafter would confine his activities to the Encyclopedia.

Father O'Connor took charge. We had always been on terms of the most cordial friendship, so there was no hitch in the office routine of publication. Then, at the end of the month, it was announced that Father Thomas J. Campbell had been appointed Editor, and the New Deal began with the issue of July 2, 1910.

Father Wynne had been Moderator of the Xavier Alumni Sodality for six years (1916-1921) and when the diamond jubilee of his entrance into the Society of Jesus—July 31, 1876—came about, it was suggested that the Sodality should make public commemoration of the occasion. On consulting him, he declined the choice of a formal dinner, and it was finally decided that the most suitable program would be an old-fashioned "Academy," at which the past fifty years would be reviewed by distinguished scholars. The date was set for the evening of December 13, 1926, at the Hotel Biltmore, and it was a grand success. Cardinal Hayes presided over an audience of several hundred, who listened to appropriate addresses from Judge John G. McTigue, President; Reverend M. A. Clarke, S.J., Moderator; Michael Williams, then Editor of the *Commonweal*; and Monsignor E. A. Pace, of the Catholic University.

Father Wynne replied in a "Retrospect," in which he outlined his career from his third year and, if the spots of exuberance were disregarded, it supplied the needed material for the future historians of his accomplishments. He had a full report of the proceedings made into a slender volume, and published with the imprint of the Sodality. A year-by-year record, from his birth, September 30, 1859, of all his various activities, to the date of the Academy, is also given.

"What an ennobling and inspiring record!" exclaims the compiler of the volume, which bears the title, *Fifty Years in Conflict and Triumph*. It certainly is the record of an extraordinary and versatile man who, in spite of what his critics may say or what they think were his defects, accomplished during one of the most progressive chapters of the Church in the United States, results that will shine out resplendent long after he has passed away.

—Thomas F. Meehan
America Staff
July 1, 1942.

It was one of the great privileges of my life to have been a protege of Mr. Meehan in my earlier years, and to know him so intimately through so many years. Here and now, I wish to state that he was one of the greatest formative influences for good in my life. In 1913, I was appointed to teach at Loyola School, New York. The Editors of *America* then formed part of the Jesuit Community on Park Avenue. Mr. Meehan apparently took a fancy to me, and I, then a young scholastic, regarded him as a wonderfully kind and extraordinary wise old gentleman. For four years, I had the opportunity of knowing the editors of *America* and Mr. Meehan.

In the summer of 1922, I was detailed as a "Summer" Editor of *America*. Under Father Tierney and his brilliant staff, I was inducted into the mysteries of editing a national Catholic weekly. Looking back now, I feel that Mr. Meehan was by my side during those summer months. First of all, he was instructing me in the mechanics of printing and editing, invaluable knowledge to

me for my later life. Then, he was trying to fill my mind with
the immense amount of knowledge that he had collected about
historical matters; he was suggesting topics about which I should
write; he was discussing the events of the day, was telling me
of his own experiences and the personages whom he had known;
and above all he was encouraging me to devote myself to a writing
career. No father woud have been kinder to any son.

The following summer, I was returned to *America* as the permanent Literary Editor, in succession to one of the sweetest geniuses,
Father Walter Dwight. Once more, Mr. Meehan took a hand
in my maturer education. Day by day, very patiently, and also
very exuberantly, he would talk about all the infinite things that
interested him. And so the friendship grew through thirteen
years until, in 1936, I was named Editor-in-Chief of *America*. I
like to think that Mr. Meehan took some pride in me, as his disciple. One of the standing jokes between us was his reluctance
to admit that I was ready to graduate as a first-class editor. But
during the six years before his death in which I was in charge
of *America* and Mr. Meehan, I was always grateful for his
intense interest in me, for his encouragement in my varied activities, for his invaluable help in so many problems, for his advice,
for his corrections and admonitions delivered gently but unmis-
takably, for his total and selfless friendship.

The personal note, which I have introduced, may be taken as
a symbol of the many other relationships between Mr. Meehan
and his friends. As he treated me, so did he treat others. He knew
the first Editors of *America* and he knew their successors through
all the intervening years. More than sixty Jesuits came and
went, and Mr. Meehan worked with them all. As each new editor came, Mr. Meehan would take him in hand and very kindly
and most unobtrusively teach him and enrich him. Some he liked
better than others. But he had a kindly word for all of them,
even though he might recall a few laughable anecdotes about them.
He had a remarkable insight into the character of men. He admired their virtues and excused their faults. He was just in his
evaluations of their capabilities and deficiencies, and he enjoyed
them all. With a twinkle in his eye, and with a wearied voice,
he would remark, with variations: "Saint Ignatius will have to

be good to me after all that I've had to suffer from his sons. They've been a bother to me ever since I can remember."

In the reverse, every editor and staff member of *America* through thirty-three years liked and enjoyed Mr. Meehan, respected and admired him, and trusted him implicitly. I, too, have known all of these Jesuits, with a few exceptions, who worked so intimately with Mr. Meehan. I have never heard one of them utter a single word of disparagement or disrespect. Always, every one of them thought of him and treated him as the ideal Catholic layman. So close did they hold him that they would have wanted him to be a Jesuit, too.

One of Mr. Meehan's best and oldest friends among the editors of *America* was Father Paul L. Blakely who died six months after Mr. Meehan, on February 26, 1943. They met in 1914, when Father Blakely was first appointed Associate Editor. No one knew Mr. Meehan better through all those years than Father Blakely. Sometime after Mr. Meehan's death, Father Blakely gave me a few pages of typing, with the remark that I might use it in writing about Mr. Meehan. It is published here, as a link between these two undoubted saints and scholars. Writes Father Blakely:

I met our beloved friend, Thomas F. Meehan, for the first time nearly thirty years ago. In the ensuing years, up to the last year of his life, I saw him almost daily, talked with him, occasionally argued with him. And every day, my esteem for Thomas F. Meehan, gentleman and scholar, increased. He wore well. There was no veneer about him; from deep sources in his soul rose the factors that made him a gentleman. His knowledge of history, especially the history of the Church in this country and, more particularly, in the city of New York, was not drawn from printed sources alone. He was a careful investigator of old documents; a diligent worker in the field of unwritten tradition. He knew what was worth knowing, and he knew it well.

Often I stopped at his desk with a question. Often, his answer developed into a lecture, detailed in flowing language that was pointed and ever piquant. That was particularly true if my question touched on some religious or political movement in New York. There was hardly an outstanding figure in the city for the last sixty years whom he did not know. Not a few, he knew intimately. He could tell you what some man prominent in Church or State said to him, or what he heard him say at some public gathering, and often from what he heard he could shrewdly deduce what they thought, but left unsaid. In his younger days, he seems to have frequented the company of men who had known the great men in the generation before them. From their lips he gathered a knowledge of historical events not set down in books and, in some cases, unfortunately, not set down yet.

Once he began to talk, Mr. Meehan was like a well full of tradition that was purified by its passage through his critical mind, and bubbled out ready for the thirsty traveler on the road of history who stopped to quaff, and ask the way to the next town. And many came to quaff.

I do not think that a week passed and, in some seasons, hardly a day, without some seeker after knowledge dropping in at Campion House, or at his home in Brooklyn, or addressing him by mail, to ask his help in indicating sources or in revising a manuscript almost ready for the press. Professors and students, priests and Nuns, and members of the Hierarchy, were his clients. To all he gave generously of his time, and the time not infrequently spread out over weeks. All were received graciously, and even the importunate and the absurd were listened to patiently and, if possible, helped.

But I remember one afternoon when his patience had been sorely taxed by a rather bumptious young man who was getting his thesis for the doctorate into shape. An important section of the inquiry dealt with a very troubled period in the history of a diocese that I leave unnamed. A journal, which ceased publication many decades ago, was an invaluable source of information on this period, and the young man informed Mr. Meehan that since he had searched in vain for the complete file, no complete file existed. There were times when Mr. Meehan could almost—but not quite—snort, and this time he just fell short of a perfect snort. "I don't know where that young man has been searching," he said to me after the visitor's departure. "But there is a complete file of that publication in the library of his own university."

Mr. Meehan's friends had often urged him to write his autobiography, yet I think there was validity in his plea of never being able to find time to write it. He was so busy helping others to write history that he had no leisure in which to write it himself. While only one published volume bears his name, I venture to think that at least a hundred are due to the inspiration and the encouragement he gave to struggling students. Not every one of these authors had the grace to remember him, but the books with prefaces which acknowledge his "invaluable aid," would overflow, I think, more than half a dozen three-foot book-cases. It would be interesting to compile a list of the books which this man, who wrote but one himself, helped others to write.

"Gentleman and scholar" is today a title that is often awarded to the unworthy. But by the strictest of all standards it belonged to Thomas F. Meehan.

PAUL L. BLAKELY, S.J.

Like testimony could be gathered from hundreds of other friends, who were equally devoted to Mr. Meehan. His years working on *America* were, in a way, quiet and hidden, but in another way brimful of excitement and stimulation. His special department was that of gathering the copy from the editors, getting it passed by the editor-in-chief, sending it to the printer, charting the proofs to the various desks, preparing the dummy, putting the paper "to bed", and then starting the preparations for the next issue.

That was merely the mechanical phase. He used to devote hours to a careful reading of the diocesan newspapers and Catholic periodicals, clipping what he thought might be of interest or value to the Staff, calling attention to articles, jotting down references covering an encyclopedic array of topics. He was invaluable because he knew everything that was occurring the present week and could tie up this knowledge with the background of the past. His fertile mind provided him with topics not only for his own frequent writings in *America,* signed and unsigned, but also for editorials and articles by the editors.

In his earlier years, he used to do a lot of contact work and confidential investigations for Father Wynne and Father Campbell and, even more so, for Father Tierney, when he was editor-in-chief. He could always be trusted to handle any matter, no matter how delicate, with tact and good judgment. In later years, with Father Parsons and myself, he preferred to devote himself more to desk work and the inner management of *America.*

During his years in the editorial office of *America,* there was only one fault he had, but it was a cultured and an inspiring fault. He loved to converse. Sometimes, in the stress of busy days the editors were not partial to talk. But it was hard to resist Mr. Meehan, for he was a very fascinating talker. Scarcely a day would pass without his discovering some new item. His whole person would glow with animation as he discussed it. His memory would toss up ramifications, and one item led to another item. It was our loss that we were hurried at times and failed to catch his fire. But he was always most understanding and always realized that, if this were not the right moment, the news would keep till another moment.

Let it not be supposed that Mr. Meehan could be boring. His talk could be lengthy but it was worth listening to and well worth recording. Looking back, it is my great regret that I did not jot down all the mass of information he poured into my mind. One never reached to the bottom of his store of knowledge. He was a continual surprise also to himself, I think, in the ramifications of his memory. Sometimes, in telling a story of some figure of a century ago, he would pause, and exclaim: "Now isn't that funny, I never thought of that before." Then, he would bring the story up to date with an account of the children and grandchildren, etc. Every conversation on an historical topic was like a complete chapter from a book.

His memory was prodigious and correct, even when he was high in his "eighties". And his knowledge he always placed at the disposal of others. He sought eagerly to help the editors in their quest for exact information. They, in turn, had never any hesitation in seeking his help, even though they knew they would be overwhelmed by the torrent of extraneous material he would draw up for them out of the deep well of his remembering.

His desk was at the crossroads of the editorial office at Campion House. Seated, there, he gave a sense of warmth to every one who passed, and a welcoming smile to everyone who paused to talk to him. He was always ready to tell about something new he had just discovered. The clipping might be in his well-stuffed wallet, or in the large envelopes he carried in his inside pocket. It might be in the drawers of his desk. That would take a little longer to find, since those drawers were stuffed to overflowing with envelopes full of clippings and letters and notes he had been making. Or else, the item would be in one of the recent diocesan papers. These he held, as if in his own preserve, in a large rack near his desk. He read all the diocesan weeklies carefully, and wanted to be the first to read them. After he had finished his weekly survey of them, he would arrange them according to his own system—he could find any one of them immediately; but the rest of us could never learn his system. But always, he would track down the account of the story he wanted to tell about.

Until just a few years back, one of the big afternoons of his week was that in which he pasted up the "dummy". This was a task in which he would brook no interference. His scissors, he told me, were more than forty years old, but they worked on the pink printer's proof. He would measure lines, ponder about space, paste it all up with an air of great tension. When new methods, looking for greater precision were introduced, he would sit back patiently and wait to be asked to help. He could always adjust himself to changes, and almost always agree that "we do things better now than we used to."

His impatience, as Father Leonard Feeney discovered, was always manifested by his leaning back in his chair, plucking at his moustache, wriggling his foot and staring at the ceiling. His irritations resulted mostly from the ignorance of someone who ought to know some historical or current fact, but just didn't know it. Then, he would reverse his usual judgment about the smartness of the young generation and conclude that the young people don't know anything and are not interested in anything.

His position on *America* was ideally teamed up with his constant labors for the United States Catholic Historical Society and its publications. He seemed to fuse his work for one and the other, to the mutual benefit of both. He was noted as an historian. But he never ceased to be an alert journalist. He loved to reminisce about the interesting characters of the past. But he was always eager to meet the newcomers who were equipped to carry on the high tradition.

Even in his "eighties", I remember him making remarks such as: "We have to get out of the old ruts. We have to do things in the modern way." Or again: "Now we have men who know how to do things. That was our trouble in the past; we didn't have people who could organize movements as we have now." Or again, as late as his eighty-sixth year, he remarked: "I've been reading Tommy's school books, history and geography.

They're wonderful. We never had anything like them in the old days. You know, some of these modern Sisters are smart. They've been educated in college and have all sorts of degrees. You never used to hear of nuns graduating from college. Now they write these textbooks, and they are good." In his admiration for the present and the younger people, he might give the impression of being irritated by the failures of the past.

To the editorial office of *America* came his visitors, from all over the country, seeking his direction and assistance in their doctoral dissertations, the books they were writing, the research they were carrying on. Most welcome to him were the Sisters who were writing historical or biographical works. He took extraordinary pride in them, and never seemed to understand how it could be that these nuns knew so much. In passing, it may be said that he looked on nuns as living saints, and championed them as would a father.

Here from the office, too, he carried on his large correspondence, spurning stenographers and typewriters, and writing with an old-type pen. Here, too, he assembled the material for the *Historical Records and Studies* and *The Monograph Series*. Issuing these books regularly was a continuous adventure for him. Each new batch of manuscripts was always something fresh and exciting, and each new printed volume was a joy and pride.

Of his own life, it is to be regretted, he wrote practically nothing. For years, his dear friend, Mrs. Rita McGoldrick, the wife of Dr. Thomas McGoldrick, his physician, kept urging him to keep a record of all the interesting memories that he spoke about. She, if anyone, could persuade him. But he would smile indulgently and try to turn the conversation. Once, she prepared a beautifully bound blank-book for him, the purpose being to make it easy for him to jot down his recollections. Waggishly, he wrote a page of dedication to her, but left the rest of the volume blank white pages.

Time and again, after listening to his marvelous memories of men and things, I, too, would urge him to settle down seriously to his autobiography. But he would never be serious about this project. When I urged him excessively, he would smile tolerantly and promise some day or other to write out something. In this, he resembled his old friend, Monsignor Michael Lavelle, for more than half a century the rector of St. Patrick's Cathedral, New York. The Monsignor, likewise, had a prodigious memory for the days that had passed, and in those days he had met the great churchmen and the great civilians. When he was about eighty, he confided to me that he was going to retire from the Cathedral in a few years, and would then write his Recollections. As his personal history of the Church passed with him, so did Mr. Meehan's. There is little need to add that our history of the Church during the past one hundred years is that much less abundant.

During the last few years of his life, his daily trips from Brooklyn to our office in uptown New York became less frequent. Much to his irritation he was forced to follow the orders of Dr. McGoldrick, and remain at home. But he never let go his interests. In my visits to him, I found that he was always riding high his enthusiasms, always discovering something that he had not known before, always rediscovering something that he had, according to him, completely forgotten, always being reminded of something that was "awfully" interesting.

Seated in his chair in the back parlor of his home on Greene Avenue with its high ceilings and tall windows and the light fading into dusk, he would talk his living history—about the visit to Archbishop Hughes, the first Archbishop of New York, at the time of the Civil War,—about the day the Cathedral was dedicated, and he was seated between General Sickles (with a long interlude about the General) and John Woods, the banker— about Cardinal Satolli (a story that has never been published but his account of it is in the Baltimore Archives)—about Father Tierney (and he also had an adventure into Spanish affairs about which I shall tell you sometime)—about the strange offer made to him to become educational director when the United States took the Philippines—and so on till the evening was spent. He was a myriad memoried man. All of us were stupid in that we failed to remember permanently his memories.

Mr. Meehan is an integral part of the history of *America*. His name will be remembered with the names of the great editors, with Father Wynne, and Father Tierney, and Father Dwight, and Father Blakely, and all others, living and dead, with whom he worked through the last thirty-three years of his life.

APPENDIX

In October 1907, the Archdiocese of New York was preparing to celebrate the centenary of the See, which would take place the following April. As their part in the plan, the *Catholic News* printed a series of notes on Catholic history in order to arouse interest in local affairs and to help preserve data which was in danger of being lost for want of permanent records.

Thomas Meehan accepted the invitation to contribute these weekly articles. Every phase of Catholic action was dwelt upon. A few of these articles are presented here to perpetuate the spirit of Thomas Meehan, the antiquarian.

SOME SOCIAL SIDE-LIGHTS

In a note printed in the last issue of the *Catholic News* Dr. Thomas Gaffney Taaffe asked if Bishop Carroll had not been entertained at a banquet given by that famous social and military organization, "The Ancient and Honorable Artillery Company," during the visit he made to Boston in September, 1803.

It was not during this visit but on the occasion of a previous one, made in the spring of 1791, that the Bishop was the recipient of this courtesy. He was invited to the annual dinner of this now oldest military organization in the country, and at the close of the banquet pronounced the thanksgiving. In writing of his reception in Boston he said: "It is wonderful to tell what great civilities have been done to me, in this town where a few years ago a Popish priest was thought to be the greatest monster in creation. Many here, even of the principal people, have acknowledged to me that they would have crossed to the opposite side of the street rather than meet a Roman Catholic some time ago. The horror which was associated with the idea of a Papist is incredible."

In his wildest dreams the good Bishop probably never once fancied that, within a century, Boston would have a Catholic Mayor and all New England be well on its way to seeing a Catholic majority in its population. The incident of the mention of this public banquet serves to recall that here in New York there were Catholics of social prominence and wealth in the early days of the last century. The local season for opera will soon open in New York, but how few know that the first Italian opera company ever brought here was by the Catholic merchant, Dominick Lynch; that Lorenzo Da Ponte, the composer of the libretti of Mozart's "Don Giovanni," "Le Nozze di Figaro" and "Cosi Fan Tutte," is buried in the old Eleventh street cemetery, and was the father-in-law of that illustrious Catholic philanthropist and scientist, Dr. Henry James Anderson, and that the prima donna of the first opera company, Maria Garcia, was married at old St. Peter's in

Barclay street during the stay of the company at the Park Theatre, which in those days faced the head of the street across Broadway.

Dominick Lynch then (November, 1825), was one of the richest merchants in New York. He lived at No. 1 Greenwich Street. He was the fourth child of Dominick Lynch, a native of Galway, Ireland, who came to New York, on June 20, 1785, from Bruges, Flanders, where he had been in business as a merchant. He had with him his wife and three children and, it is claimed, the largest amount of cash money that had up to that time been brought to New York by any individual. He went into partnership with Dom Tomas Stoughton, afterwards for thirty years consul here for Spain. They were merchants and importers at No. 26 Greenwich Street. Lynch took up his residence at No. 36 Broadway. Don Diego Gardoqui, the Spanish minister, lived next door, and the next house was that occupied by President Washington when he lived here in 1790. This row is described by Col. John May in his journal, under date of April 22, 1788, as "the finest buildings my eyes ever beheld, and I believe they excel any on the continent." The Stoughtons lived at No. 75 Leonard Street. Both Lynch and Stoughton were prominent in the founding of St. Peter's Church, and the firm advanced the money by which the purchase of the lots in Barclay Street was made from the Trinity Church trustees. Lynch not only made a generous personal contribution to the church building but wrote to his relatives and friends in Ireland asking their assistance. He was the founder of the present city of Rome, New York, having in 1786-88, purchased about 2,000 acres of land on the Mohawk River now covered by that city, which he first called Lynchville, the name Rome not being given to it till some years later. In 1790 when the Catholics of the United States sent an address of congratulation to President Washington, he was one of the four laymen who signed it. In 1797 he purchased a country seat in Westchester County, on Long Island Sound, where he built a spacious residence. This is now the property of the Christian Brothers who use it as a part of their academy for boys. It is known today as Clason-on-the-Sound. Dominick Lynch called it Woodlawn and there he died in his seventy-first year, on June 5, 1825. He was buried in the family vault in old St. Patrick's, Mulberry Street. Ten children were born to him in this city. Most of them made mixed marriages and their descendants are now outside the Church. They are to be found in the Tillotson, Shippen, Luqueer, Pringle, Orr, Olin, Lawrence, Lea, Norton, Maitland, Harvey, Canby, Ridgway, and other New York families.

Dominick Lynch, Jr., was educated at Georgetown. He made many trips to Europe and during one of them persuaded Manuel Garcia, in 1825, to bring over New York's first Italian opera company from London. In "The Old Merchants of New York" it is said of him that he "coined money and spent it with the freedom of a prince." He had a lovely family of daughters and bought a place on Staten Island next door to the Pavillon Hotel at New Brighton, where he lived until he died in 1844. He never saved anything and consequently died poor.

Another prominent merchant of this period was Cornelius Heeney, who was born in Kings County, Ireland, in 1754, and came later penniless when thirty years of age. He was employed as bookkeeper in the fur store of William Backhous, No. 40, Littel Dock (now Water Street), where John Jacob Astor, the founder of the family of the present-day millionaires, was a porter. Backhous retired from business and left the store to his two employees, who prospered in it for several years. Then they separated and opened individual establishments, Heeney at 82 Water Street. He lived over the store, as was the custom in those days, with two bachelor friends, Francis Cooper and John George Gottsberger, both of whom were prominent for years in Catholic affairs. Heeney was also a bachelor and devoted much of his fast increasing wealth to works of piety and charity. It is estimated that he gave in cash and real estate to various New York institutions and churches more than $60,000, which was an immense sum in those days. He served for five terms, 1818 to 1822, in the State Assembly, being one of the first Catholics elected to office in New York.

When the great fire of 1835 destroyed his Water Street store he retired from business and went to live in Brooklyn where he had purchased a plot of seventeen acres in 1806 for $7,500, that is now included by Congress and Amity Streets, Court Street and the East River. Here he lived dispensing his charities with lavish hand. He gave the site for St. Paul's Church and the asylum and school adjoining it. Two years before his death he planned to have his whole estate, as he had its income, go to charity, and accordingly he secured from the Legislature, May 19, 1845, an act incorporating "The Trustees and Associates of the Brooklyn Benevolent Society." To this corporation he transferred his real and personal estate to be administered for the benefit of the poor. The income of this property now amounts to $25,000 a year, and more than a million dollars has been distributed since Mr. Heeney died. It costs only about 5 per cent, to administer it, the rest going in charity as Mr. Heeney directed. The first trustees were Cornelius Heeney, Francis Cooper, James Friel, Henry M. Pachem, John George Gottsberger, Noel J. Becar, William F. Peck, Peter Turner and Bartlett Smith, with the Bishop of the diocese of New York and the Mayor of Brooklyn as ex-officio members. The "associates are those who contribute three dollars a year and all officers and trustees serve without pay except the Treasurer and Agent, who have small salaries." Mr. Heeney supervised the operations of the Society until shortly before his death, which took place in his ninety-fourth year on May 3, 1848. Few of the present generation can tell who he was or why his name should be held in grateful recollection by the Catholics of New York. Unlike most of the rich men who make large charitable bequests he obliterated his own personality in the selection of the title "The Brooklyn Benevolent Society." During his residence in New York he was specially generous to old St. Peter's in Barclay Street. The pews and gallery fittings removed in the recent reconstruction of this church were his gifts. He brought the first Sisters of Charity here from Emmitsburg in 1812 to take care of the Prince Street orphan asylum, to establish which he gave $18,000 and donations of land. He built the free school for girls and the half orphan asylum for St. Patrick's parish, and gave one of the lots that went to enlarge its graveyard.

Lorenzo Da Ponte was the son of a Jew leather dealer named Jeremiah Conegliano, of Ceneda, Italy, and was called Emmanuel until his fourteenth year, when with the rest of the family he was baptized a Christian in the Cathedral of Ceneda on Aug. 20, 1763. The Bishop of the See, taking a fancy to the boy, whose brilliant mind had already manifested itself, gave him his own name and sent him to school to the Diocesan seminary. Here he remained for five years. He then got into political troubles and went to Vienna, where he met Mozart and wrote the libretti of the famous operas. After a varied career there and in London, he came to New York, June 4, 1805. Here he spent most of his subsequent days as a teacher of Italian. He was the first teacher and commentator in America on Dante's "Divine Comedy." He died at No. 91 Spring Street on August 17, 1838, was buried in the old Eleventh Street cemetery in a grave that cannot now be located. His daughter was married to Doctor Henry James Anderson, founder of the Catholic Protectory and for so many years President of the Catholic Union and the St. Vincent de Paul Society. Edward Henry and S. Ellery Anderson, the well-known Democratic lawyer, were their sons. Dr. Anderson was a convert, but Edward Henry alone followed his example.

OUR FIRST NEWSPAPER

When the Rev. William O'Brien Pardow was appointed recently to the rectorship of St. Ignatius' Church mention was made of the fact that his grandfather, Robert Pardow, was one of the proprietors of New York's first distinctively Catholic paper, *The Truth Teller,* the publication of which began on Saturday, April 2, 1825. The progress of Catholic journalism and publications makes a most interesting chapter of our local history.

The first newspaper in which Catholicism and topics of Irish interest, but not religious matters exclusively, were the leading features called *The Shamrock* or *Hibernian Chronicle.* It was a weekly started by Thomas O'Conor, father of the eminent jurist, Charles O'Conor, December 10, 1810, and ceased to be published August 17, 1817. It was revived as a monthly magazine called *The Globe* in 1819 and this lasted about a year.

Thomas O'Conor was a member of the ancient Irish family of that name and was born in Dublin in 1770. He died in the city in his eighty-fifth year. He came here in 1801, was associated with William Kernan and others in establishing a settlement in Steuben County, New York, and his name occurs frequently in the early records of St. Peter's and St. Patrick's parishes. His son, Charles O'Conor, writing of him on Feb. 25, 1867, says:

"I think he never aspired to the character of an author. He first resorted to his pen as a means of earning a scanty subsistence for his family. This must have been about the year 1811. He was connected with the press at intervals thenceforward until he had reached a very advanced age. . . .

"He was a devoted Catholic, an enthusiastically patriotic Irishman. . . . Whether employed in procuring bread for his family or in the freely chosen pursuits of easy leisure, his pen was always under the influence of these sentiments. It was ever directed in vindicating the fame of Ireland, the honor of our United American States, or the truth and purity of his cherished Mother, the Apostolic Church."

Early in 1812 he was the editor for several months of a weekly paper called *The War*. In September of the same year, with Stephen Wall, he began the publication of a journal called *The Military Monitor* which preceded *The Shamrock,* but both these papers were purely secular and their inception was caused by the incidents of the War of 1812.

The first number of *The Truth Teller* is dated April 2, 1825, and bears this imprint:

"New York: Published regularly every Saturday by W. E. Andrews & Co. at the office of the Truth Teller, 95 Maiden Lane, where communications (post-paid) are respectfully requested to be directed. Terms, Four dollars per annum—payable half yearly in advance. Subscriptions and Advertisements will be received at the office of the Truth Teller, Mr. J. Costigan's Catholic Book Store, 17 Chatham Street, by Mr. P. Connolly, General Agent; Mr. B. McKenna, Agent for New York, Brooklyn and the surrounding neighborhood, and by the following agents. . . . Printed by M. Toohey and J. McLoughlin, 11 Spruce Street."

It was an eight-page paper, 10 x 14 inches, printed in large, clear type in three wide columns. There is not one word of local Catholic news in the first five issues. In the sixth, that of May 7, appears the first mention of local Catholicism, the announcement that on the following day a charity sermon would be preached by the Rev. Dr. John Power in St. Patrick's Cathedral for the building of an orphan asylum under the care of the Roman Catholic Benevolent Society. The first page of the initial number is devoted to a long "Address," which explains why the paper was started, mainly a scoring of the English press because of their circulation of untruths about the Catholic Church and the people of Ireland. Six columns are devoted to the proceedings of the Catholic Association, in Dublin, at meetings held two months before—this, it must be remembered, was the time when if often took that long for the mails to cross the Atlantic—and to a debate in the House of Commons on the same association about the same date.

The imprint "W. E. Andrews & Co." appears on the first six issues of the paper, then it is dropped, and no publisher's name is given until the paper of Oct. 29, when "Printed by the Proprietors, George Pardow and William Denman, at the office Collect opposite Canal Street," appears. The publication office remained at No. 95 Maiden Lane. In the paper of Jan. 2, 1830, George Pardow states that he has disposed of his interest in the concern to William Denman, under whose management it was continued until March 31, 1855, when Denman sold *The Truth Teller* to Patrick Lynch and William L. Cole, proprietors of *The Irish American*. They published it for a short time as a separate paper and then merged it in *The Irish American.*

The connection of "W. E. Andrews" with the publication opens up a chapter of international history of which very few seem to be aware and which points to him as the inspiration of the first two Catholic papers in the United States, Bishop England's *Catholic Miscellany,* of Charleston, begun in 1822, and the New York *Truth Teller,* in 1825. William Eusebius Andrews was one of the most active and noted publicists and writers in the England of the eventful period of the last century that witnessed the successful Battle for Catholic Emancipation. He was the right-hand man of the famous Bishop Milner and an indefatigable and indomitable publisher of Catholic literature. Born at Norwich, Dec. 6, 1773, he died at London, April 7, 1837. His parents were converts, and he began his career as a printer's apprentice in the office of the *Norfolk Chronicle,* of which paper he was afterwards editor from 1789 to 1813. In the latter year he went to London and began there his remarkable life of activity in the cause of Catholic journalism and literature. Among the publications he started were *The Orthodox Journal* and *Catholic Monthly Intelligencer* (1813) under the auspices of Bishop Milner; *The Catholic Vindicator* (Glasgow, 1820); *The Catholic Advocate of Civil and Religious Liberty* (1820); *The Catholic Miscellany* and *The People's Advocate* (both 1822); *The Truth Teller* (1824), and several subsequent papers up to 1836. Most of all these were short-lived but no sooner did one stop than he began another under a new title. He fell out with O'Connell over some of the details of the fight for Emancipation, and used his *London Truth Teller* for continued and vigorous assaults on the policy of "The Liberator." This, of course, made him very unpopular with Irish Catholics, and is perhaps the reason why we have little or nothing about him in our records. He published a number of books, pamphlets and tracts, editing (1818) that once most popular book, Bishop Milner's, *End of Controversy.*

George Pardow and William Denman were both English, but there is nothing at present available to explain the exact connection of Andrews with the starting of the *New York Truth Teller,* or what he contributed to the enterprise thus launched under his name. That he was intimate with its conductors is shown in several instances. Thus in the paper dated May 14, 1825, is quoted an "article from the pen of Mr. Andrews, the London editor. It gives such a just and correct view of the state of the affairs of the Catholics of Ireland, and coming from a person so well qualified, being on the spot, to form a correct judgment, that we cannot deny ourselves the pleasure of inserting it for the benefit of our readers."

Again in the paper of September 10, 1825, there is a notice headed "important," which goes on to say: "In order to counteract the injurious effects produced against Catholics by pretended reports from private correspondents in Paris sending over the calumnies and false statements which appearing in the English papers are copied with avidity into the Prints of this country, we have in conjunction with Mr. Andrews of the *London*

Truth Teller, established a correspondence with a Catholic gentleman, residing in Paris in every way qualified for the task, who will from time to time transmit true and correct statements of the state of affairs more particularly in regard to Religion in France and on the Continent." The first letter, under date of Paris, July 21, is then printed. This goes to show that there was some journalistic enterprise in those days and that the syndicate methods of today, on which we so often pride ourselves, and the equally often asserted need of a reliable Catholic news agency in Europe to offset the fakes and lies of the secular press, were both anticipated by our first Catholic paper eighty-two years ago. The satisfactory remedy for these evils, however, does not seem to have been entirely supplied even at this late date.

Consideration of the personality of the publishers of the *Truth Teller* and some of the notable local contributors to its first issues is of interest here.

George Pardow was a scion of an old English Catholic family and was born near Birmingham, February 26, 1772. He married Elizabeth Seaton November 18, 1799, and they had ten children, six boys and four girls. Of these, six, three girls and three boys, were living when the family came to New York in 1823. Mr. Pardow had been in the hardware business in England, and here his chief trade was in needles which in those days, before the era of the sewing machine, were a very important item of domestic economy. His store was at No. 95 Maiden Lane, and the family lived in Green Street. He was also among those who were first to introduce the then new-fangled steel pens which gradually superseded the old-fashioned quills. From the start he was active in Catholic affairs. His name is to be found in the list of subscribers to the New Testament, which the Reverend Dr. Power of St. Peter's published in 1824. He was for a number of years a trustee of St. Peter's, and his name occurs constantly among those prominent in all the Church affairs of the time. He died April 7, 1846. His wife died on June 16, 1841, aged sixty-one years. They were both buried in old St. Patrick's churchyard.

Of all their children, Gregory Bryan, who was the eldest son, and Robert, were sent to Stonyhurst, the famous English Jesuit college to be educated. Gregory entered there January 14, 1817, and Robert, September 6, 1821. Gregory also studied in Rome and at St. Mary's Baltimore. He was ordained priest here in New York by Bishop Dubois, September 8, 1829, and is described as an elegant writer and preacher but of delicate health. He was the first pastor resident at Newark, New Jersey, serving there from 1829 to 1832. He was stationed at Albany in 1836 and 1837, and died, aged thirty-four years, April 24, 1838. His sister Julia entered the Convent of the Sacred Heart, Dec. 15, 1845, and took the veil as a religious of the Sacred Heart on Jan. 2, 1846. She was superior for several years of the convent that used to be in West Seventeenth Street. She died Sept. 22, 1857. Another sister, Helen, married Mr. Edward Mullen and after his death joined the Sisters of Mercy on June 23, 1854. She died as

Mother Teresa in the old Convent of Mercy, No. 35 East Houston Street, January 1876.

Robert Pardow, their brother, married a daughter of William O'Brien who was a banker and one of the interesting figures of New York society a century ago. She died on May 18, 1870. Robert Pardow was a well-known business man in this city up to the time of his death, May 11, 1882. Two of his daughters are Madame Augusta and Madame Pauline Pardow of the Sacred Heart order. His son is the well-known Jesuit, the Rev. William O'Brien Pardow, rector of St. Ignatius Church. Another son, Robert was a Wall Street broker and went to the Civil War with the Twenty-second Regiment. He married Miss Kate Carrigan on July 31, 1866. When she died, March 30, 1873, he also joined the Jesuits and after the usual course was ordained priest. He died at St. Francis Xavier's on May 8, 1884, of disease contracted during his tour of duty as chaplain at the Charity Hospital, Blackwell's Island.

William Denman, who was George Pardow's partner in the publication of the *Truth Teller* at its start, was a curious character, a low-sized, small man in stature and without any special literary ability. He usually wore a military cloak and called himself "Major," but even as early as 1832 his right to this title seems to have been questioned. He was born in Edinburgh, Scotland, March 17, 1784. His father was a German and his mother an Alsatian. He claimed to have been in the British army and to have been wounded at the battle of Waterloo. The Catholics in New York when the *Truth Teller* was started were nearly all of Irish birth or kin, and Denman became a local political figure owing to the prominence and influence his position as owner of a Catholic paper gave him. He devoted more of its space to Irish and political topics than he did to religious matters and was tainted with the prevailing errors of trusteeism. Rival papers were started, the *Weekly Register* in 1832, the *Catholic Register* in 1839, the *Freeman's Journal* in 1840, and others, before whose competition the circulation and prestige of the *Truth Teller* waned.

He married the daughter of an Austrian officer named De Monti. Mrs. Denman died at the family residence in James Street in 1847 and was buried in old St. Patrick's. They had twelve children, five of whom—four sons and a daughter lived to maturity. The sons were educated at St. John's, Fordham, West Point and Annapolis. The daughter Mary Elizabeth went to St. Joseph's, Emmitsburg, Md. She married John Colgan and died in 1868. Three of the sons were in the United States service. Adjutant Frederick J. Denman, of the artillery was accidentally killed in Texas in 1854. Acting Ensign Joseph A. Denman of the U. S. Navy, died in 1862. Charles L. Denman was commissioned from West Point to the Eleventh Regiment and served in the Mexican war. In May, 1853, President Pierce appointed him consul at Acapulec, Mexico. He was later, for many years, attached to the New York and Brooklyn post-offices. He died in Brooklyn on March 17, 1893, aged 80 years. William Denman, the youngest son, worked on the *Truth Teller,* and was later for some time editor of the

New York Tablet. The old Major, their father, outlived all his day and generation and died on September 12, 1870, in Brooklyn. He had spent most of the very last years of his long life, unknown and forgotten, in the family of a generous friend, the late Mrs. James Coleman, who was a sister of William O'Brien the California "Bonanza" millionaire.

In the promotion of the publication of the *Truth Teller* the Very Rev. Dr. John Power, rector of St. Peter's was very active. Dr. Power was born near Roscarberry, County Cork, Ireland, June 19, 1792. He was educated at Maynooth and for some time was a professor at the Cork Diocesan Seminary. In 1819, the trustees of St. Peter's as was the custom in that time, brought him to New York. He was made pastor there and Vicar-General by Bishop Connolly and he acted as administrator during the period between the death of that prelate and the advent of Bishop Dubois. He was an eloquent preacher, a man of fine literary tastes and a pious and zealous priest and missionary. His admirers thought that his abilities ought to have been rewarded with a miller. Bishop Purcell, writing from Cincinnati, on Oct. 9, 1834, to Bishop England of Charleston, in regard to a coadjutor for the latter, who had been charged by the Holy See with a mission to reform the Church in Haiti, says:

"I expected, if you have nothing better in petto for him to see our friend John Power of New York among the men according to your own heart. I fear his merits are not sufficiently appreciated where he is."

Dr. Power died April 14, 1849, his last days saddened by the mismanagement of the church affairs by the trustees. He was buried in the vaults of old St. Patrick's. Dr. Power's brother married a Miss Livingston, who had a large fortune, and they went back to Ireland to enjoy it. Another brother was a physician long and well known on the East Side in old St. Patrick's parish.

In many of the early numbers of the *Truth Teller* are contributions signed "Berkley MacAlpin," which was the favorite pen name of the Rev. Thomas C. Levins, who was one of Dr. Power's assistant at St. Peter's and at St. Patrick's. He was born at Drogheda, County Louth, Ireland, March 14, 1789. He studied at Clongoes and at Stonyhurst and entering the Society of Jesus he was sent to Georgetown in 1822. He remained from July 22, 1822, to March 6, 1825, when he left the Jesuits. He came to New York on the invitation of Dr. Power and officiated at St. Peter's and at St. Patrick's. He was a learned and vigorous writer with special mathematical talents and gifted as theologian and controversalist. He was twice named as a member of the Board of Visitors to the West Point Academy. He had a testy temper and a strong spirit of insubordination. This it was that led to his leaving the Jesuits by a violation of the strict rule of censorship of all literary productions that governs the members of the Society. It also brought him into conflict with Bishop Dubois, in October, 1834, and he was suspended from his priestly functions. He was very popular among the people of St. Patrick's parish and the trustees sided with him against the Bishop and refused to recognize the successor the Bishop named in his place. A very bitter conflict waged for a short time, when Father Levins, who was otherwise irreproachable in his conduct, retired from the field. He spent several years in literary pursuits and had his faculties restored by the Bishop in 1841, when he was given a charge at Albany. His sight soon after this failed and he came back to St. Peter's where he died of paralysis May 5, 1843.

Father Joseph A. Scheneller, another contributor, was also a former Jesuit scholastic who was ordained here by Bishop Dubois on Dec. 24, 1827. With Father Levins he started and ran the *Weekly Register,* a rival to the *Truth Teller,* from October 5, 1833 to 1836. In 1828 he was stationed at St. Peter's Church, Anna Street, 1833-35; St. James, 1835-37; St. Mary's Albany, 1838-46; St. Paul's, Brooklyn, 1846-September 18, 1862, when he died. Father Scheneller was a native of Germany, a staunch advocate of Catholic education, and by his vigorous pamphlets and articles in the press did much to refute the innumerable calumnies against Catholics circulated by the fanatics of the time.

Other contributors to the *Truth Teller* were the venerable Thomas O'Connor, father of the great lawyer, Charles O'Connor; Dr. William J. Macnevan, the Irish patriot of 1798, whose memorial is to be seen in St. Paul's churchyard on Broadway (he was not buried there) ; Thomas S. Brady, father of Judge John R. Brady and James T. Brady, the famous politician and lawyer.

SOME NOTABLE CONVERTS

Early in the year 1816 the Rev. Benedict J. Fenwick, S.J., of St. Peter's, who was acting as Vicar-General and administrator of the diocese of New York pending the arrival of the new Bishop, Dr. Connolly, from Rome, received a visit at his house, No. 15 Jay Street, from an Episcopalian clergyman, who introduced himself as the Rev. Virgil Horace Barber, president of the academy of that denomination located at Fairfield near Utica, N. Y. Mr. Barber was in search of information concerning the doctrines of the Catholic Church and the solution of many doubts that had arisen in his mind about the truth of the religion of which he was a minister. From this visit resulted a series of the most remarkable conversions, having a wide-reaching effect on the progress of the faith in New England. We get some interesting personal details of them from the letters and diaries of the Barber family, and other data collected by the late Bishop De Goesbriand for his "Catholic Memoirs of Vermont and New Hampshire."

Virgil Horace Barber was the son of Daniel Barber, a soldier of the Revolution, who was born at Simsbury, Conn., Oct. 2, 1756. In early life Daniel Barber was a Congregationalist, but later became a minister in 1787, at Schenectady, N. Y., by Bishop Provost. In a "History of My Own Times," which he printed in Washington, D. C., in 1827, he says some of his mother's people must have been Catholics, for "I well remember my mother's habit of signing each loaf of bread with the sign of the cross before it was put into the oven for baking, and the same was the practice of many others. My mother could give no other reason for this than because the same was done by her mother, and, although this sign had its proper meaning as well as its origin, of both she was ignorant, and although the sign had lost its meaning, still the habit of using it had become so confirmed as seeming to claim its right by possession." He served two terms of enlistment in the Continental army and about the year 1787 moved from Connecticut to the village of Claremont, N. H., where he was settled as the minister of the local Episcopalian church, and remained in charge there for twenty-four years. In 1807 he baptized Fanny Allen, who subsequently became a convert and a nun at the Convent of the Hotel Dieu, Montreal (Sept. 29, 1808) the sixth woman of New England birth and ancestry to become a religious.

During her stay in Montreal the Rev. Daniel Barber visited her and was present at her profession (1810). He was much impressed by what he saw and by her piety. Some Catholic books he read after this gave him serious doubts as to the validity of the orders he had received at his ordination. "Wishing for information on that subject," he says, "led me to introduce myself to the Rev. Dr. Cheverus, then a priest in Boston. He treated me with great candor. He gave me an understanding of the principal things which made the separation between us and the Catholic Church. He also furnished me with several books to carry home. These proved quite a treat in my family. They, by reading, soon appeared well convinced of the truths they contained and wished to see a priest, but the nearest was a hundred miles distant. These few books scattered fast among my Protestant neighbors, and those more particularly who had a taste for inquiry." Among these books was Milner's, *End of Controversy.*

Virgil was Daniel Barber's youngest son, and, as stated above, had followed his father into the ministry, being then the head of the Episcopalian academy at Fairfield, N. Y., where he was living at the time with his wife Jerusha, and his three daughters. He had in his family an Irish servant girl, and one day he found her reading *A Novena to St. Francis Xavier.* He borrowed the book, and the short life of the saint it contained affected him greatly and led to his obtaining a more extended one. The book fascinated him. "Night and day he kept it by him," says his daughter in her memoir of her mother, "even under his pillow, read and reread it himself and to my mother, and even to the Episcopal Bishop and ministers; and often, too, offended my mother a little by saying his parallel could not be found in the whole Protestant Church." A son was born to him at this time and he wished to call him Francis Xavier. His wife objected that she would have "no Popish names in our family," and after some further dispute called the boy Samuel. She lived to see this son a Jesuit. About this time Virgil Barber and his wife visited his father in New Hampshire, and when they left carried back to New York some of the books given to Daniel Barber by Dr. Cheverus of Boston. They studied them attentively, and after much anxiety and research, in which the wife was made to share every exploration and discovery, he with her approval resolved to visit New York City for the purpose of consulting the books to be found in the library of St. Paul's Church (Broadway and Fulton Street). He stayed a week in the city, and it was then that he called on Father Fenwick, S.J., who was attached to St. Peter's, Barclay Street, and living at No. 15 Jay Street.

The Jesuit found him open and candid and manifesting a sincere desire to know the truth. In the course of the conversation he learned who his visitor was, and the position he held at the academy and seminary at Fairfield. His inquiries were answered and Father Fenwick gave him several books to study, and on a request for permission to call again at some future day, earnestly invited him to come back whenever he felt so inclined, and entreated him to pursue his investigations, Mr. Barber then went back to Fairfield to his wife and school.

"Night after night," says his daughter in her memoir, "my parents used to sit up together, discussing points of doctrine and reading works of controversy. . . . But as it became more evident to my parents that they must quit the side of error, and as they openly expressed to the Protestant Bishop and ministers their sense of the insecurity in their communion, the latter made every effort to retain them in their old faith. Several discussions were held in our house. . . . My father at least was perfectly satisfied; my mother not sufficiently so as yet. I was born just about this time and the first prayer my mother ever addressed to the Blessed Virgin was on my account. She promised that if she would deign to assist her in her hour of need she would believe in and pray to her. She experienced the help desired. This was Aug. 9, 1816. The day following the professors and trustees of the college came to make a last effort at reclaiming my father. My mother, knowing they would debate points of controversy and anxious to hear all they had to say in defence of either side of the question, requested the conference might be held in an apartment adjoining her bedroom. She had the door left ajar so that she could hear every word; and there during the one or two hours the disputation lasted heard all the arguments of the ministers refuted by my father."

Mr. Barber paid another visit to New York and called again on Father Fenwick, who received him cordially. All that occurred during the several months since the previous visit was gone over, and the visitor admitted that the Protestant faith could no longer be defended and seemed greatly at a loss what to do. The care of his family—he then had five children and the predicament in which he would be placed filled him with apprehension, but Father Fenwick consoled him, advised him to embrace the truth as he had found it and leave the rest to God. He further advised him to go back to Fairfield, resign his ministry in the Episcopalian church, settle his affairs as soon as he could and return to New York, where a new school would be secured for him and made as successful as possible. A few days after he agreed to this he was formally received into the Church and returned to Fairfield, where he informed his congregation of his change of faith and bade them a final adieu. They turned against him to a man, and in the face of such prejudice he wound up his affairs and began preparations to leave for New York with his wife and their five children, Mary the eldest, born January 1810, Abigail in 1811, Susan in 1813, Samuel in 1814, and Josephine, a babe in arms. This was in the fall of 1816.

When they reached New York, Father Fenwick received them with open arms and kept them in his own house until he secured a new one for them at No. 24 Vesey Street, in which the proposed school was opened. This was a success from the start and a number of children joined his classes. Mrs. Barber was soon after baptized, as were also the children. In the diary she kept are these entries:

"Dec. 24, 1816—Josephine baptized by the Rev. Mr. Fenwick at his house, Jay Street, No. 15, New York City."

"Feb. 9, 1817—Mr. B. and myself made our first Communion at 8 o'clock in St. Peter's chapel, Barclay Street."

In the record of her mother's life Josephine says: "Being settled in New York my father applied himself at once to the business he had come upon and applied to the Catholic clergy, who seemed to look upon him with some distrust. The Rev. B. Fenwick, however, seemed to penetrate the uprightness and earnestness of his purpose and to take in it a friendly interest. My father was accustomed to go to the Catholic church to Mass, Vespers, etc., and was frequently accompanied by some of the other Episcopal ministers. One in particular agreed with him in admiring and approving of everything he saw and heard, doctrine as well as ceremonies, whereupon my father asked why, then, did he not become a Catholic. 'My family,' said he, 'are the only obstacle. I would have no means of maintaining them.' After my father's death my mother used to relate this to me, and with tears rolling down her cheeks; assuring me at the same time that they were tears not of grief but of joy and thankfulness to God that by His grace no such consideration had prevented her husband from following the truth."

The Barber school at No. 24 Vesey Street lasted less than a year, for after the family had been here for a short time as Catholics both husband and wife began to aspire higher to a degree of perfection and to consecrate themselves entirely to the services of God by separating and entering a religious life. After talking the project over Mrs. Barber consulted their friend, Father Fenwick, on its possibility, assuring him that, "if the matter can be accomplished with justice to the children she was in every way desirous of it." Barber was then thirty-four years of age, his wife twenty-eight and the five children eight, seven, five, and three years and the baby eight months respectfully.

Father Fenwick was astonished at this proposal and at the moment saw no way of meeting it. He counselled Mrs. Barber to give it up, because the children, having no means of support away from their parents, would, if a separation took place, necessarily suffer. Bishop Connolly then arrived in New York and Father Fenwick returned to Georgetown and the Jesuit

foundation in New York was abandoned for the time. Before he left, however, he recommended the Barber family strongly to the new Bishop. A
short time, after Father Fenwick reached Georgetown he received a letter
from Mr. Barber recalling his attention to the religious life ideas, expressing his great longing to become a Jesuit and asking if something could
not be done for him at Georgetown. The rector there at that time was one
of the famous men of the lately restored order, Father John Grassi, and
Archbishop Neale, of Baltimore, was living at the Visitation Convent in
Georgetown. In a house near by Mrs. Fenwick, Father Fenwick's mother,
was living, so that she could be close to her sons, three of whom became
Jesuits. After explaining the conversion of the Barbers and their present
desire to separate to enter a religious life, he gained the consent of these
three important factors to the project. Father Grassi agreed to receive
Mr. Barber as a novice into the Jesuit community and his six-year old
son, Samuel, as a student into Georgetown College. Archbishop Neale
consented to the reception of Mrs. Barber into the Visitation Convent as
a nun and of the three elder daughters, Mary, Abigail and Susan, as pupils
of the school. Mrs. Fenwick was to take the ten-months old baby Josephine,
and care for her until she also was old enough to go to the convent school.
The venerable Mother Teresa Lalor was then the head of the Visitation
community.

These arrangements were communicated to the family in New York and
early in June 1817, the school in Vesey street having been closed and their
affairs here settled up, Mr. and Mrs. Barber and the five children set out
for Georgetown. On arriving there they went to Mrs. Fenwick's house.
Several wealthy Catholics offered to adopt the children, but the mother
refused to alter the arrangement already made. They remained at the
Fenwick mansion until June 21 when the formal separation took place.
Father Grassi invited Mrs. Barber to dine in the refectory of the college,
a privilege never before granted to any woman. After this they all re-
paired to the college chapel, where Archbishop Neale, in presence of a
number of the clergy and laity, received Mr. and Mrs. Barber's individual
assents to the decree of separation and they renounced each other. Mr.
Barber and the little Samuel went into the College. Mrs. Barber and three
of her daughters were conducted to the Visitation Convent, and the baby
Josephine was given in to the motherly care of Mrs. Fenwick.

Mrs. Barber was then twenty-eight years old and so eager was she to
begin her novitiate that without waiting for the ceremony of formal in-
vestiture she made herself a complete religious dress and put it on without
ado, much to the surprise of the community, who were amused at her simplicity and earnestness. She was finally given the habit on July 26, 1817,
taking the name of Sister M. Augustine. Soon, however, a new trial be-
fell her. Some of the Sisters fearing that it was not yet proper to admit
her into the convent, she was forced to leave on Oct. 24th for a period of
probation, and remained out at the residence of Mrs. Lewis in Baltimore,
until the 14th of April following, when she was again received into the
Georgetown community.

Shortly after Mr. Barber joined the Jesuits at Georgetown. Father John Grassi, the rector, was called to Rome, and Father Fenwick succeeded him as head of the college. Father Grassi set out on June 28, and took with him to Rome Mr. Barber and three other scholastics. They were most kindly received in Rome, and were presented to Pope Pius VII. After an absence of a year Mr. Barber returned to Georgetown and pursued his theological studies there. On Feb. 2, 1820, nearly three years after their separation, husband and wife met again in the Georgetown convent chapel to make their vows. Mrs. Barber first went through the formula of profession as a Visitation nun and then Mr. Barber made his vows as a Jesuit novice. Their five children were present; Mary the eldest being ten years old and Josephine, the youngest, two and a half years. Thereafter, Mrs. Barber in her letters and diary speaks of her husband as "Brother Heirome." He went to Boston after finishing his studies at Georgetown and was ordained priest by Bishop Cheverus on Dec. 3, 1822. After his return from Rome in 1818 he paid a visit to his old home at Claremont, N. H., bringing with him Father Charles French, the Dominican, who had been acting as pastor at St. Peter's, Barclay Street, New York. They remained at Daniel Barber's house for a week, Father French celebrating Mass several times—the first ever said in that section—and preaching a sort of mission. The result was the conversion of old Mrs. Barber, Daniel's wife; Mrs. Tyler, his sister; her husband and their four sons and four daughters. Of these sons, William, then sixteen years old, became the first Catholic Bishop of Hartford, Conn., and the four daughters all joined the Sisters of Charity at Emmitsburg, Md. Sarah, who entered in 1827 lived to be nearly one hundred years of age. Daniel Barber, the father was not baptized with his wife, but was entered into the church some time later at Georgetown. He resigned his charge as Episcopalian minister of Claremont, Nov. 12, 1818. He spent most of his later life, his wife dying, near his son, Virgil, and died at St. Inigoes, Md., in 1834. He was buried in the cemetery of the mission house of the Jesuits there. In his early manhood he was one of the volunteers who joined the Continental army from Connecticut after the battle of Bunker Hill and he participated in the siege of Boston. He was with his regiment during the engagements about New York, but had to leave it on account of ill health after the battle of Long Island.

When Mrs. Barber entered the Visitation Convent the school was in special need of such an addition to its teaching force. She had received an excellent education and was a woman of tireless energy and zeal. She taught the children's classes during the day, and in the evening and during recreation drilled the Sisters in methods of teaching and in the branches in which they were deficient. She was in time made directress and under her management its reputation grew steadily. Previous to this, however, the community had a very hard time, and such was its poverty that at one time, in 1822, being in want of the very necessaries of life, the Sisters had determined to disband, and give up the effort to establish a branch of the Visitation order.

They were saved from this by the generosity of a New York merchant, John Baptist La Sal whose name is to be found frequently in all the records concerning the early years of old St. Patrick's, especially the orphan asylum and schools. His place of business was at No. 224 Front Street and he lived at No. 49 East Broadway. Wishing to send his daughters to a convent school he went to Georgetown to arrange for their reception, and arrived just at the time when the school was in its direst need. Touched by its poverty, he insisted on advancing a sum of money that paid the tuition for several years of his three daughters and his sister, and thus saved the existence of the institution. The La Sal girls who were educated at Georgetown were Charlotte, Virginia and Louise. Charlotte, the eldest, was eight years old when she entered the school, where she displayed remarkable talents, graduating with the highest honors nine years later. She then returned to New York, and a gay life of fashion seemed her only ambition. It led to an indolent disregard of her religious duties.

In this she was but following the example of her father, who although most charitable and generous in the material affairs of the church, had for years neglected the sacraments. She continued in this state of indifference until a serious illness interrupted her gayety. At the same time she received a letter announcing that a favorite classmate was about to join the Georgetown community. This made so great an impression on her that she determined to abandon the world herself. Her father for a long time refused his consent, but finally was won over, and 1836 brought her back to the Georgetown convent, where she received the veil and took his name, becoming in religion Sister Baptista. She only lived a year, dying on April 9, 1837, and making her final vows on her death-bed. Before she died she got her father to promise that he would receive Holy Communion for her after her death. He kept the promise, went to the Jesuit college at Georgetown, made a retreat and received the sacraments, which he had not approached for twenty-two years.

The addition of the Barber children to the Georgetown community at the time it was in such financial straits was a cause of much suffering to their mother—or Sister M. Augustine as she was called—as she knew many of the Sisters were much opposed to their remaining a burden on the house.

"She has told me that many a time," writes her daughter, Sister Josephine, "she sat up nearly half the night patching her children's clothes (for she at this time had charge of the school) and knitting stockings for them; and that on cold winter mornings when the girls were going to Mass she used frequently to take down from the window an old baize curtain to throw about Abby's or Susan's shoulders they having no shawl or cloak.

"Nearly all the clothes," said she, "were made of what the other girls threw away. Polly Spalding adopted one of you and made you new dresses out of her old ones. When you were in need of shoes we used to go to the pile where the girls' old ones were thrown away and select the best from among them for you. Sometimes they were so large that you could hardly walk in them. You had not always sheets on your beds; and in winter when your bedclothes were insufficient I used to cover you with the other girls' cloaks and shawls. Once when Mary had the measles very bad I could not get the proper nourishment for her. These and other things were owing to the poverty of the house and not to any unkindness on the part of the charitable Sisters; nevertheless they kept my mind in a constant state of suffering. Good Father Cloriviere, old Mother Teresa and Sister Agnes were, however, very kind and did for you all in their power. I would put myself under the feet of any one who would do anything for my children."

When Josephine was about two years old Mrs. Fenwick, her guardian, took her to the convent to see her mother. The nun extended her arms to take the child, who was told, "This is your mother, Josephine." But the child refused to leave her nurse and exclaimed: "No, she is not." When she was taken back to the Fenwick home her mother went to her room and began to weep bitterly, and Sister Agnes, the mistress of novices asked her why she was crying. "My God, My God!" answered the novice, "to think that my own child does not know me!"

On Nov. 14, 1825, Mr. Barber was in Georgetown and saw his wife and children all together for the last time. The meeting was a tearful and sorrowful one. In the following April, as then arranged, Mary went to enter the Ursuline convent at Boston and Abby that at Quebec. In 1827 Susan and Josephine also left, the former for the Ursuline convent at Three Rivers, Canada, and the latter for the Ursuline convent in Boston. In 1832, Samuel, the son, made his vows as a Jesuit novice at Whitemarsh, Md. The whole family was now enrolled as religious, and then Mrs. Barber gave her daughter this explanation of its incentive:

"Previous to my marriage," she said, "being extremely anxious to obtain the consent of my family to the union and apprehending opposition from several of them I had recourse to God and repeatedly promised Him if He would only grant your father to me I would give him back gladly again and all my children likewise if I had any. Twenty times a day did I throw myself on my knees and reiterate this promise, not comprehending fully the purport of what I said nor imagining the sense in which God heard it; but I have always believed that this promise was the foundation of the religious vocation of our family."

Mrs. Barber remained at Georgetown convent until the summer of 1836, where she was sent West to a new house of the Visitation order, founded three years before at Kaskaskia. Here she remained until 1844, when she was sent to St. Louis, Mo. She was transferred from St. Louis to the convent at Mobile, Ala., then much in need of teachers, in the summer of 1848. In the winter of 1855 she was attacked by a serious illness, and her daughter, Sister Josephine, was sent for to take her place in the school. She recovered from this attack, but in the following year she was again laid up and consumption developed. She was confined to the infirmary for two years and died on January 1, 1860, her daughter being with her all during her last illness. She was buried in the convent cemetery.

After his ordination by Bishop Cheverus in 1822, Father Virgil Barber went back to his old home at Claremont, N. H., and began his work for the conversion of his former companions and neighbors. With the aid of his father and contributions he gathered in Canada, where he spent most of the winter of 1824, he built a small church adjoining his father's house, with which he connected it, and opened there an academy, which soon became very popular. Three of his pupils who later became famous in the Church in New England were William Tyler, James Fittan and William Wiley. His venerable father used to help in the school and served his daily Mass. His mother died here in 1825, consoled by the ministrations of her son. In addition to his work at Claremont, Father Barber, at the request of the Bishop, also served as a missionary among the Indians of Maine until January, 1829, when his superiors recalled him to Georgetown. Bishop Fenwick, seriously grieved at this loss to his very sparsely equipped diocese, asked that Father Barber should be allowed to remain in charge of the Indian missions. The request was granted, and he returned to work among the Penobscot and Pasamaquoddy tribes in the following May and remained there for some time.

He then returned to Georgetown and was stationed at different times at Frederick, Caughnawaga or some other of the Jesuit houses of the Maryland Province. He died at Georgetown of paralysis after an illness of two years in March, 1847. His father followed him to Maryland and had the privilege of going from one house to another of the order in Maryland and Pennsylvania to be near him. The Old Catholic families there were also glad to have him as a visitor. As a soldier of the Revolution he received a small pension. He died, as before stated, at St. Inigoes, Md., in 1834, aged seventy-eight years.

During his residence in Maryland, Father Barber often saw his wife until she was sent West to the convent at Kaskaskia, Ill., in 1836. Their last interview took place in Baltimore, while she was en route there at the convent of the Sisters of Charity, of which his cousin, Sister Genevieve Tyler, was Sister Servant.

"This last severance from her seemed to open a new wound in his soul and to renew the pangs of former years," says his daughter. "Though separated he had had the comfort of seeing her at the grate and feeling himself sustained spiritually and mentally by the words of holy and cheerful encouragement she spoke as well as by her promise of prayers in his behalf. This had been to him a stay even in the world; but now it must be relinquished too. It was a hard trial to him during the last ten years of his life and to her likewise. Once while at Georgetown she got permission from the Archbishop and Mother N. to make a general confession of her whole life to him, thinking that she could speak to him more freely and importune him with more questions and explanations than she could venture to trouble any other priest with. She accordingly prepared and wrote her confession, and on his next visit invited him into the church under some pretext or other without mentioning her real object. When they reached the sacristy she informed him of the permission she had obtained and the preparation she had made. He replied that he would listen to all she had to say and answer all her questions but not by way of confession, and I believe he satisfied her fully. She remained, I think, about a week in Baltimore during which time my father visited her frequently, until Father Borgna (Bishop Rosati's vicar-general, who had come East to bring the Sisters back to Kaskaskia) returned from Georgetown, when they took their last adieu, and my mother resumed her journey towards the far West."

Samuel Joseph Barber, their son, after making his preparatory studies at Georgetown College entered the Society of Jesus, making his vows as a novice at White Marsh, Md., Aug. 15, 1832. He was then eighteen years old. During the same summer he went to Rome in company with Father McSherry and the subsequent Father Samuel Mulledy. He remained abroad eight years, and having been ordained priest returned to Georgetown, where he filled with ability and success the offices of vice-president and professor. He was also master of novices at Frederick, pastor of St. Thomas Manor, Charles County, Md., and resident of Gonzaga College, Washington, D. C. He died at St. Thomas Manor, Feb. 23, 1864, aged fifty years. During his stay in Rome he acted for a time as prefect in the College of the Nobles in addition to pursuing his own studies at the Roman College.

In a letter to his mother from Rome, dated April 19, 1825, he says of the famous Jesuit so well known in the early years of the Church in New York: "Father Kohlman, whom I see oftener this year than before, shows great affection towards the whole family and speaks often of father and mother. He has become old and his limbs tremble a great deal, but nevertheless he still labors much for the conversion of souls, insomuch that he has not a spare moment." Father Kohlman, it will be remembered, was called to Rome to teach in the Roman College after leaving New York.

Mary, the eldest child of Virgil Barber was born in January, 1810. She spent several years with her mother at the Visitation convent in Georgetown and then went to the Ursuline convent at Charlestown, near Boston, where she took the veil as Sister Mary Benedicta, Aug. 15, 1826. She made her profession two years later. When the Charlestown convent was burned by the mob of anti-Catholic fanatics in 1834, and the project of re-establishing the school was abandoned, she went with the other members of the community to the house of the same order at Quebec, where she died on May 9, 1848. She taught the classes in English literature. She has left a graphic narrative of the destruction of the Charlestown convent.

Abigail, the next daughter, accompanied her sister to Boston, and after a short stay there continued on to Quebec, where she entered the Ursuline convent as Sister Francis Xavier. On Sept. 11, 1878, she celebrated the golden jubilee of her religious profession. In the following November she had a stroke of paralysis which left her speechless for some time. She recovered a little but died on March 2, aged sixty-nine years.

Susan Barber was born Jan. 4, 1813, at New Haven, Conn. She entered the school of the Ursuline convent at Three Rivers, Canada, May 21, 1830. As her education was well advanced she was received into the order on Dec. 8, of the same year. She took the white veil and the name of Sister Mary Joseph, March 19, 1831, and made her profession March 19, 1833. She died there Jan. 24, 1837.

Josephine, the last of the daughters who was a baby entrusted to Mrs. Fenwick when her parents entered a religious life, went with Susan to the Urusline convent in Boston in 1827, but returned to Georgetown later and entered the Visitation order.

"My health not being very good in the autumn of 1830," she writes, "Mother St. George sent me to Cornish, N. H., to spend some months in the family of Capt. Bela Chase, brother of Mother M. Ursula Chase (converts). The family was a saintly one; they said morning and night prayers. . . . On Sunday they recited the whole catechism and . . . chanted the Mass not only through devotion, but in order to retain what they had learned and to teach their children the same; for there was then no priest at Claremont, but one from Burlington visited the station three months, lodging at Capt. Chase's, where an apartment was always kept for him. I had been here a few weeks only when my father's arrival was announced. He had come on some business matter and stayed two nights and a day— the only two nights I had slept under the same roof with him from infancy. Wishing to profit by the opportunity of going to confession, I several times withdrew to prepare, but could not stay away from my father. At length I was obliged to give up the idea of confession, and my father left. After his departure, as I was expressing my regret for having missed the oppor- tunity, Mrs. Chase told me to write to him, for he was staying for a few days with his brother at Claremont (six miles distant), and would return if I solicited it. I wrote, and meantime made my preparation. Next day I sat at the front window and watched for the mail coach—not a steam car, but drawn by four horses. As I saw them turning toward the front gate my heart beat with joy; my father got out, and in a few hours after- wards I had the happiness of making my confession—the first I had ever made to him. Capt. Chase and all the family (except the oldest son) went also. After they were all through I went back to the parlor, and my father, who seemed more delighted than I was myself, took me up under the arms and jumped me several times half-way to the ceiling, exclaiming: 'My baby! My baby!' I was fifteen and very slight. My father, on the contrary, was remarkably tall and stout, portly and handsome. He always called me his baby because I was the youngest."

Sister Josephine remained in the Visitation community at Georgetown, which she had joined, until 1833, when she went West with the other Sisters who founded the convent at Kaskaskia. On her way there they stopped over at Frederick, Md., where she again met her father and wished to go to confession to him. "I asked Mother Agnes' permission to go to Holy Communion likewise," she writes, "but she said as the Sisters were not going I had better not. Of course I obeyed, but have always regretted the privation, as although I assisted at my father's Mass I never had the happiness of receiving Holy Communion from his hands. Two hours after this the stage coach stood at the door and I bade my father a last and long farewell. In parting he put into my hand a paper which I did not open until we were far up among the mountains. It was a little poem, beginning thus, 'God call thee hence, my darling child.' My father after helping in all the Sisters, closed the coach door. One more word of adieu and we were on our way Westward. My father stood on the pavement watching the stage coach as it receded with the last of his five children, and I too looked out at him as long as he remained in sight. . . . Three years afterward my mother came out West."

In 1856, when her mother, who was then at the convent in Mobile, was taken ill, Sister Josephine was sent for to take her place as a teacher, and remained there until after her mother's death, which took place, as before stated, January 1, 1860.

The conversion of the Rev. Virgil H. Barber in New York produced other results in the same direction, as it paved the way to the entrance into the Church of the Rev. Dr. Kewley, rector of St. George's Episcopalian church; the Rev. George E. Ironside, also an Episcopalian, and the Rev. Calvin White, of Connecticut. The latter was the grandfather of the architect, Stanford White, recently murdered in this city, and the father of Richard White, the writer. None of Mr. White's family followed him into the Church. The Rev. John Richards, a Methodist preacher in the western part of New York, was so zealous in his efforts that he went to Montreal with the intention of converting the Sulpicians there from the error of their ways. The result of it was that he was converted himself, entered the seminary and was ordained priest, July 25, 1813. He died on July 23, 1847, in Montreal of typhus fever caught while ministering to some unfortunate Irish immigrants. An interesting and rare little book printed in Brooklyn 1809, on the episode is "An Inquiry into the Fundamental Principles of Roman Catholics in a Letter to Mr. John Richards, by Samuel Coate."

Another notable conversion was that of Colonel Dodge, of Pompey, New York, one of the most prominent men in Onondaga county. He and his wife were devout Presbyterians. One stormy night in the winter of 1836 an Irish peddler, Francis Murphy, who lived in Utica, while on his way to Cazenovia with a sleigh load of goods he had purchased in New York City, stuck in a snowdrift, in front of Colonel Dodge's house. The latter and his son came out and helped the peddler out of the drift, and as the night was very stormy and the road very bad, invited him in to spend the night. After supper the conversation grew controversial, and as the peddler was well posted in his religion, he was able to answer all Col. Dodge's objections to Catholicity. In the morning when he was leaving he gave his host a copy of Milner's, *End of Controversy* and promised to send him other Catholic books. As a result Colonel Dodge and all his family became converts. In fact some twenty conversions took place in this vicinity.

Colonel Dodge's daughter, Mary C. Dodge, was well known to two generations of Catholic women of this city she helped to educate. She became a Sister of Charity, entering the old Mt. St. Vincent Convent, which is now the restaurant building Central Park, in February, 1853, taking the name in religion of Sister Maria. It is hardly necessary to recall her energy of character and executive ability to old New Yorkers who had occasion to meet her during the many subsequent years in which she filled the offices of secretary and treasurer of the corporation and directress of the Academy of Mt. St. Vincent-on-the-Hudson. She died there suddenly of heart disease on January 15, 1893.

Mr. and Mrs. Barber's separation and entrance into religious orders was not the only instance of the kind during that era. The Rev. John Austin, a Dominican missionary in Ohio from 1822, to 1828, had been an officer in the English army who was converted with his family and his sister. The latter and his wife entered a community of English, Augustinian nuns in Belgium, and he became a Dominican. He died at Canton, Ohio, in 1828.

Another case, which, however, did not have so happy an ending, was that of the Rev. Pierce Connelly, an Episcopalian minister of radical Puseyite tendencies, who officiated at Natchez, Mississippi, in 1827. His wife became a Catholic at New Orleans in 1836, and soon after both sailed for Europe, where at Rome he followed her example in March of the same year. They both wished to enter a religious life, but were persuaded to wait for some time. They returned to America, where they spent several years in retirement. Then they went back to Rome and after much insistence were allowed to separate in 1844. Mrs. Connelly entered a convent of the Sacred Heart and her husband went to a seminary and was ordained a priest two years later. He tried to become a Jesuit but was denied admission into the society.

Mrs. Connelly then left the community of the Sacred Heart and went to England to found an education establishment in a house offered her by the Earl of Shrewsbury, who also made the Reverend Mr. Connelly his private chaplain. The latter was ambitious and wanted to become a Bishop. His vanity in this direction not being satisfied, he gradually lapsed back into Protestantism and then applied to the English courts to give him back his wife. She, however, refused to break her religious vows and continued steadfast in her community life. The court proceedings created a great scandal in 1849 and 1850.

BIBLIOGRAPHY

The following is a list of the literary productions of Thomas F. Meehan arranged alphabetically according to the periodicals in which they appeared and chronologically according to their appearances.

America,   "The Census and the Churches," April 24, 1909.
"   "L'Enfant and the Capital," May 1, 1909.
"   "History of the City of New York in the Seventeenth Century," June 26, 1909.
"   "Diplomatic Intercourse with the Vatican," July 17, 1909.
"   "The Old California Missions," July 24, 1909.
"   "The Irish Pioneers of New York City," July 31, 1909.
"   "Letters to the Editor of *America*," August 7, 1909.
"   "A Memory of the 'Black '47'," August 14, 1909.
"   "The Catholic Hudson River," September 25, 1909.
"   "United States Ministers to the Holy See," October 2, 1909.
"   "Colleges for Catholic Girls," May 21, 1910.
"   "Some Catholic Chaplains," June 18, 1910.
"   "The First Catholic Fourth of July," July 2, 1910.
"   "Australia's Venerable Primate," October 1, 1910.
"   "Margaret Brent—The First Suffragette," December 17, 1910.
"   "American Nuns Abroad," April 11, 1914.
"   "Soul-hunting in Brooklyn," May 16, 1914.
"   "The Damnable Iniquity of Proselyting," June 13, 1914.
"   "Catholic Landmarks of New York," October 31, 1914.
"   "An Early Transaction in Cotton," November 21, 1914.
"   "Old St. Patrick's, New York," May 1, 1915.
"   "What Happened, July 4, 1776," July 3, 1915.
"   "A Century of Catholic Weeklies," September 11, 1915.
"   "Historical Records & Studies," Vol. VIII, November 27, 1915.
"   "The New International Encyclopedia," Vols. XIII-XVI, January 1, 1916.
"   "Pioneer Sisters' Friends," March 4, 1916.
"   "The New International Encyclopedia," Vols. XVII-XVIII (Book Review), March 11, 1916.
"   "Correct Ecclesiastical Titles," April 29, 1916.
"   "The Ever Neutral Flag," June 24, 1916.
"   "The Genesis of Barclay Street," August 12, 1916.
"   "Archbishop Hughes on Prison Discipline," October 28, 1916.
"   "156 Fifth Avenue," November 25, 1916.
"   "The Editor of the *Dublin Review*," December 23, 1916.

" "A Coming Tercentenary Celebration," January 13, 1917.
" "Two Great Women—Undesirable Immigrants," March 3, 1917.
" "History of Mother Seton's Daughters," McCann, (Book Review), March 24, 1917.
" "A Memorial of Andrew J. Shipman," (Book Review), June 16, 1917.
" "Thomas Maurice Mulry," June 30, 1917.
" "The Red Cross and Its Antecedents," July 28, 1917.
" "Literature for Soldiers," September 8, 1917.
" "Catholic Encyclopedia and Its Makers," (Book Review), November 3, 1917.
" "Very Rev. Charles Hyacinth McKenna, O.P., V.G." by V. F. O'Donnell, (Book Review), November 10, 1917.
" "Our First Army and Navy Chaplains," December 8, 1917.
" "The Patron and the Destroyer Jacob Jones," December 22, 1917.
" "Catholic Chaplains in the Mexican War," February 23, 1918.
" "Irish not Catholic," March 23, 1918.
" "Catholic Books and Public Libraries," March 30, 1918.
" "Our First Catholic Editor," March 30, 1918.
" "Life of John Cardinal McCloskey," by Cardinal Farley, (Book Review), April 6, 1918.
" "Mother Seton's Baptism," April 6, 1918.
" "War-Time Notes About Archbishop Hughes," April 13, 1918.
" "Mother Seton's Baptism," May 4, 1918.
" "Army Statistics of the Civil War," July 6, 1918.
" "A Moylan Outside the Fold," August 3, 1918.
" "The Passing of a Journalistic Landmark," August 10, 1918.
" "Aircraft & Submarines," August 24, 1918.
" "Illinois Catholic Historical Review," (Book Review), August 31, 1918.
" "India and the Future," (Book Review), September 28, 1918.
" "Teaching Catholic History," November 23, 1918.
" "An Echo from the Past," November 30, 1918.
" "Historic Mackinac," Edwin O. Wood (Book Review), December 7, 1918.
' "The First American-born Nun," December 14, 1918.
" "Some American Catholic History," January 11, 1919.
" "Historical Gaucheries," January 18, 1919.

"   "Washington and Anti-Irish Propaganda," February 9, 1919.

"   "New York's First Native Bishop," March 15, 1919.

"   "A Problem in Catholic Statistics," April 12, 1919.

"   "Story of the Irish in Argentina," Thomas Murray, (Book Review), December 13, 1919.

"   "James Danatien Le Roy de Chaumont," May 29, 1920.

"   "The Oldest Catholic School for Women," July 24, 1920.

"   "Chronicles of America Series," Johnson, (Book Review), August 21, 1920.

"   "Some of the Debt Due Catholic Austria," December 4, 1920.

"   "Mrs. MacSwiney & Carroll of Carrollton," December 18, 1920.

"   "Chronicles of Clan Carthy," April 23, 1921.

"   "An Early New York Petronius," November 12, 1921.

"   "The 'Diaries' of Wilfrid Scawen Blunt," February 18, 1922.

"   "The Inaugurator of Our Parish School System," March 11, 1922.

"   "The Dream of Rosine Parmentier," January 19, 1924.

"   "Two Pioneer Russian Missionaries," February 2, 1924.

"   "The New American Cardinals," March 22, 1924.

"   "Our First Catholic School for Girls," May 24, 1924.

"   "A Catholic Note on Poe's 'Raven'," June 28, 1924.

"   "A Day in Greenwich Village," August 16, 1924.

"   "The First Holy Name Society," September 6, 1924.

"   "Fifth Avenue, New York, 100 Years Old," October 18, 1924.

"   "Maurice Francis Egan's Memoirs," November 15, 1924.

"   "Archbishop Hughes, Some Personal Traits," January 3, 1925.

"   "St. Patrick's Day Musings," March 14, 1925.

"   "The Truth Teller: A Centenary," April 4, 1925.

"   "Thomas D'Arcy McGee," April 18, 1925.

"   "Bishop McQuaid of Rochester," July 11, 1925.

"   "A Voice from the Past," August 1, 1925.

"   "President Pierce and Pius IX," August 29, 1925.

"   "Federating Our Catholic Alumni," October 31, 1925.

"   "Galway and the Opera," November 28, 1925.

"   "Wanted: A Catholic Census," March 27, 1926.

"   "New York's First Catholic Office Holder," April 10, 1926.

"   "Bishop McQuaid's Life and Letters," August 14, 1926.

"   "Helping Calles Victims," September 25, 1926.

"   "A Famous Catholic Landmark Passes," July 30, 1927.

" "Back of Old St. Peter's, New York," August 13, 1927.

" "The Next Eucharistic Congress," September 24, 1927.

" "The New World's Oldest Book," December 10, 1927.

" "American Loans to the Pope," March 10, 1928.

" "The First Catholic Daily," May 26, 1928.

" "The Unbreakable Grip of a 'Dead Hand'," September 8, 1928.

" "Archbishop Hughes and Mexico," September 29, 1928.

" "New York Honors the Pope's Flag," March 2, 1929.

" "The Centenary of American Catholic Fiction," April 6, 1929.

" "John Jacob Astor's Partner," May 4, 1929.

" "America and Catholic Emancipation," June 22, 1929.

" "An Airport's Catholic Tradition," June 29, 1929.

" "DeTocqueville's American Advisers," March 7, 1931.

" "Washington and the Catholic Press," March 5, 1932.

" "The House of Sadlier," June 4, 1932.

" "Pilgrimages to Rome and Lourdes," August 19, 1933.

" "Our First Native-born Priest," October 13, 1934.

" "Pioneers of the Catholic Press," March 16, 1935.

" "Catholic Action, Bible Readers and Publishers," January 16, 1937.

" "Some Bible and Catholic Press Month Notes," February 13, 1937.

" "Maurice Francis Egan: Writer, Teacher, Diplomat," April 3, 1937.

" "A Century Ago Two Visitors Describe New York," May 8, 1937.

" "Catholic Women Writers: Who Was Our First?" June 5, 1937.

" "Long Links to Italy for Miss Byles Going to Perugia," August 28, 1937.

" "Our Oldest Catholic Weekly Relinquishes Its Individuality," October 2, 1937.

" "Veteran's Note on Libraries," December 4, 1937.

" "Premature Report Starts Some Catholic Press History," December 18, 1937.

" "Curious Cullings from a Once Important Review," April 2, 1938.

" "Horse and Buggy Letters; Their Culture in a Bygone Era," July 2, 1938.

" "Chaplain Service of the Navy and Army," September 17, 1938.

" "Records & Studies of America's Catholic Past," November 12, 1938.

"   "Catholic Press Association Harks Back Half a Century," June 24, 1939.

"   "Maine Layman Wins Remembrance," October 28, 1939.

"   "Our First Consul to the Papal Court," January 20, 1940.

"   "Soldier's Charm," January 27, 1940.

"   "Editors and Magazines Have Always Had Troubles," April 13, 1940.

"   "Who Are Catholics—How Can They Be Numbered?" May 4, 1940.

"   "Draft Riots of the Civil War," November 9, 1940.

"   "Add 156 to Fordham's Century," November 30, 1940.

"   "Early Shamrocks," March 15, 1941.

"   "Pierre Toussaint, Negro Catholic," June 28, 1941.

"   "Fifty Years Ago (A Postscript)," August 2, 1941.

"   "Oldest Shrines to St. Patrick," March 14, 1942.

Americana
Encyclopedia
Year Book,   "Roman Catholic Church," 1924.

"   "Roman Catholic Church," 1925.

"   "Roman Catholic Church," 1926.

"   "Roman Catholic Church," 1927.

"   "Roman Catholic Church," 1928.

Brooklyn Citizen,   "Calvary Cemetery—The Great Catholic City of the Dead," November 4, 1886.

"   "Pater Noster Row"—A Curious Phase of New York Life—The Publishing Business in Barclay Street, June 12, 1887.

"   "St. Patrick's Society": History of First Irish Social Organization, April 1, 1888.

Brooklyn Daily
Eagle,   "100 Years of Roman Catholic Church in New York City," April 28, 1908.

"   Letter—"The Pope and the Comet," April 13, 1914.

"   "Cradle of Catholic Brooklyn Still Stands at York and Gold Streets." First Mass in 1822, September 29, 1918.

"   "Early Catholic Landmarks in Brooklyn, Which Have Vanished with the March of Time," November 3, 1918.

"   Letter—correcting Catholic historical dates in, "An Historical Parochial School," January 29, 1921.

"   "The New York Emmets," January 15, 1922.

"   Letter to Heffernan. Reply—"Bowing to Superior Authority." Feb. 11, 1940.

The Catholic
Encyclopedia,   Allen, Edward Patrick, Volume I.
   "   Amat, Thaddeus, Volume I.
   "   Anderson, Henry James, Volume I.
   "   Athenry, Volume II.
   "   Bacon, David William, Volume II.
   "   Baker City, Diocese of, Volume II.
   "   Barber Family, The, Volume II.
   "   Barron, Edward, Volume II.
   "   Barry, John, Bishop of Savannah, Volume II.
   "   Barry, Patrick, Volume II.
   "   Bayer, Adele, Volume II.
   "   Bayley, James Roosevelt, Volume II.
   "   Beauregard, Pierre Gustave Toutant, Volume II.
   "   Becker, Thomas Andrew, Volume II.
   "   Bedford, Henry, Volume II.
   "   Benziger, Joseph Charles, Volume II.
   "   Blanc, Anthony, Volume II.
   "   Bon Secours, Institute of, Volume II.
   "   Borgess, Caspar Henry, Volume II.
   "   Boston, Archdiocese of, Volume II.
   "   Bradley, Denis Mary, Volume II.
   "   Brondel, John Baptist, Volume II.
   "   Brooklyn, Diocese of, Volume II.
   "   Burns, James, Volume III.
   "   Burlington, Diocese of, Volume III.
   "   Byrne, Andrew, Volume III.
   "   Byrne, Richard, Volume III.
   "   Byrne, William, Volume III.
   "   Carroll, Daniel, Volume III.
   "   Catholic Benevolent Legion, Volume III.
   "   Cavanagh, James, Volume III.
   "   Congresses, Catholic, Part III, Volume IV.
   "   Corcoran, Michael, Volume IV.
   "   Cosgrove, Henry, Volume IV.
   "   Cosin, Henry, Volume IV.
   "   Croke, Thomas William, Volume IV.
   "   Cummings, Jeremiah Williams, Volume IV.
   "   Da Ponte, Lorenzo, Volume IV.
   "   Day, Sir John, Volume IV.
   "   Denman, William, Volume IV.
   "   Detroit, Diocese of, Volume IV.
   "   Directories, Catholic (United States), Volume V.
   "   Donahue, Patrick, Volume V.
   "   Dornin, Bernard and Thomas Aloysius, Volume V.
   "   Ducoudray, Philippe-Charles, Volume V.

"   Marquette League, Volume IX.
"   Meagher, Thomas Francis, Volume X.
"   Monroe, James, Volume X.
"   Mulhall, Michael George, Volume X.
"   Mulholland, St. Clair Augustine, Volume X.
"   Mullanphy, John, Volume X.
"   Murray, John O'Kane, Volume X.
"   Newark, Diocese of, Volume XI.
"   Oertel, John James Maximilian, Volume XI.
"   O'Hara, Theodore, Volume XI.
"   O'Higgins, Ambrose Bernard, Volume XI.
"   O'Reilly, Bernard, Volume XI.
"   O'Rorke, Patrick Henry, Volume XI.
"   Parmentier, Antoine-Augustine, Volume XI.
"   Periodical Literature, Catholic, United States, Volume
         XI.
"   Peter, Sarah, Volume XI.
"   Rosecrans, William Stark, Volume XIII.
"   Sadlier, Mary Anne Madden, Volume XIII.
"   Sands, Benjamin and James, Volume XIII.
"   San Francisco, Archdiocese of, Volume XIII.
"   Scammon, Ellakim Parker, Volume XIII.
"   Semmes, Raphael, Volume XIII.
"   Sheridan, Philip-Henry, Volume XIII.
"   Sullivan, Peter John, Volume XIV.
"   Tenney, William Jewett, Volume XIV.
"   Thanksgiving Day, Volume XIV.
"   Thayer, John, Volume XIV.
"   Truth Societies, Catholic; in Ireland, Australia; United
"   States, Volume XV.
"   Verrazano, Giovanni da, Volume XV.
"   Walsh, Patrick, Volume XV.
"   Walsh, Robert, Volume XV.
"   Ward, James Harman, Volume XV.
"   Webb, Benjamin Joseph, Volume XV.
"   White, Charles Ignatius, Volume XV.

Catholic
Historical   "A Self-effaced Philanthropist—Cornelius Heeney, 1754-
Review,   1848," Volume IV, April, 1918.
"   Comments on "Early Catholic Publications," Volume
                    IV, April 1918.
"   "Catholic Literary New York (1800-1840)," Volume IV,
                    January 1919.
"   Review of *Doctrina Breve,* Volume V, 1920.
"   Review of Bixby's "P. Sailly," Volume VI, 1920.

Catholic
Messenger,   "First Cardinal in the United States," April 1910.

Catholic Mind,   "Catholic New York,"
     "   "Some Landmarks of the Faith, Cathedrals, Churches, Institutions—Statistics," June ?. 1924 (whole pamphlet).

Catholic News,   "To Boston a Century Ago," October 5, 1907.
     "   "The Jesuits in New York," October 12, 1907.
     "   "Some Early Parishes, Buildings,"
          St. Peter's Rectory & Academy,
          St. Nicholas on 2nd Street,
          Transfiguration,
          St. Andrews, Duane Street,
          Franciscans, Sullivan Street, October 19, 1907.
     "   "Some Social Side-lights,"
          The Stoughtons,
          Dominic Lynch,
          Cornelius Heeney,
          Lorenzo DaPonte,
          Dr. Henry James Anderson, October 26, 1907.
     "   "A Famous German Pioneer," Very Rev. John Raffeiner, November 2, 1907.
     "   "Old St. Michael's Church," November 9, 1907.
     "   "A Little Romance and Tragedy," Mrs. Seton, November 16, 1907.
     "   "Our First Newspaper," November 23, 1907.
     "   "Our First Newspaper," continued with a consideration of the personality of the publishers of *The Truth Teller* and some of the notable local contributors to its first issue, George Pardow and William Denman, November 30, 1907.
     "   "Some Notable Conversions," The Famous Barber Family, December 7, 14, 21, 28, 1907.
     "   "An Almost Forgotten Scientist," Andrew Parmentier, January 4, 1908.
     "   "The Graves of the Dead," "Trinity,"—"St. Paul's,"—"St. Patrick's"—"Old 11th Street", January 11, 1908.
     "   "St. Patrick's,"—"Old 11th Street," January 18, 1908.
     "   "About the Cathedral," St. Patrick's, January 25, 1908.
     "   "The New Cathedral Site," February 1, 1908.
     "   "The Eleventh Street Cemetery," February 8, 1908.
     "   "Care of the Orphans," R. C. Orphan Society, R. C. Half-Orphan, February 15, 1908.
     "   "Donations of Public Lands," February 22, 1908.

"	"The Sisters of Charity," with extracts from *The Truth Teller,* July 30, 1830,—February 29, 1908.
"	"Some Material Incidents," March 7, 1908.
"	"St. Patrick's Day Celebrations," March 14, 1908.
"	"Chaplains and War Time Incidents," March 21, 1908.
"	"Publishers and Book Sellers," Barclay Street, N. Y., March 28, 1908.
"	"Schools and Teachers," The Early Catholic Schools of New York, April 4, 1908.
"	"Editors and Newspapers," April 11, 1908.
"	"Editors and Newspapers," April 18, 1908.
"	"The Diocese of New York," April 25, 1908.
"	"The Pardow Family in New York," January 30, 1909.
"	"Foundation of Ursuline Nuns," March 6, 1909.
"	"Centenary of the Sisters of Charity," November 27, 1909.
"	"Life Story of a Remarkable Woman," Mother Mary Aloysia Hardey, November 10, 1910.
"	"K of C in Peace and War," May 15, 1920.
"	"Pilgrim's Foes of Religious Liberty," November 13, 1920.
"	"The Truth Regarding St. Patrick's Title Deeds," told by One Who Knows, December 16, 1939.
Catholic Northwest Progress,	"What,—Is That Old Lie Up Again?"—Civil War Desertion, July 19, 1918.
Catholic World,	"The First American Cardinal," Volume XC, March, 1910.
"	"Catholic Activities in Our Two Great Wars," Volume CVII, July, 1918.
"	"Official Catholic Directory," Volume CXXVI, January, 1928.
"	"The Fellow Traveler," Jubilee Edition, April, 1940.
Columbia,	"Barry—Father of the American Navy," October 1922.
"	"Paying Our Debt to Italy," August, 1922.
"	"The Mirrors of Barclay Street," December, 1923.
Commonweal,	"Word Shadows of the Great," Volume XII, September 10, 1930.
"	"Worker in Gold," Volume XIII, February 25, 1931.
"	"America's First Italian Opera," Volume XIII, April 1, 1931.

The Messenger, "Italian Missions," January 1903.

The Monitor, "Organization of the Catholic Church in the United States," November 7, 1908.

National Catholic Welfare Council, "Charles O'Conor, First Catholic Nominated for Presidency, Bondsman of Jefferson Davis," May, 1927.

New International Encyclopedia, "Franciscans," Volume V.
" "Roman Catholic Church," Volume IX.

New International Encyclopedia Year Book, "Roman Catholic Church," 1920.
" "Roman Catholic Church," 1925.
" "Roman Catholic Church," 1929.
" "Roman Catholic Church," 1930.
" "Roman Catholic Church," 1931.
" "Roman Catholic Church," 1932.
" "Roman Catholic Church," 1933.

The New York Herald, "Musical 'Cops' of the Opera Squad," February 28, 1904
" "Romance of Parmentier Family Revived by Death ot Last Member," January 30, 1908.

The New York Sun, "Letter About the Early Dates of New York Tablet," June 21, 1912.
" "Macneven and Emmet," August 14, 1916.
" Letter—"Henry James Anderson," February 2, 1917.

The North American Review, "Organization of the Catholic Church in the United States," November 1908.

Our Lady of Lourdes Booklet, (Washington Heights) "Pilgrimages to Lourdes," October 1933.

The Republic, "New York's Next Archbishop," September 6, 1902.
" "New York's 'Lily of Churches' and Archbishop Hughes," October 1, 1910.

The Tablet,	"Catholic Brooklyn in 1834,"
"	"Catholic Journalism in New York City," April 1, 1933.
"	"Book Presents Some Novel Brooklyn History," (Tia Barbarita: Memoirs of Barbara Peart), February 24, 1934.
"	"Cradle of Catholic Brooklyn," April 21, 1934.
"	"Catholic Brooklyn A Century Ago," November 1941.

The United States Catholic Historical Society (Records & Studies)

"Archbishop Hughes and the Draft Riots," Volume I, 1899.

" "Joseph W. Carroll," Volume I, 1899.

" "Pioneer Times in Brooklyn," Volume II, 1900.

" "Bishop Loughlin As a Citizen," Volume II, 1900.

" "Some Schools in Old New York," Volume II, 1900.

" "New York's First Catholic Newspaper," Volume III, 1903.

" "The First Charity Concert for the Catholic Orphans of New York," Volume III, 1903.

" "Andrew Parmentier, Horticulturist, and His Daughter, Madam Bayer," Volume III, 1903.

" "Some Pioneer Catholic Laymen in New York—Dominic Lynch and Cornelius Heeney," Volume IV, 1906.

" "Rev. Denis Paul O'Flynn," Volume IV, 1906.

" "Henry James Anderson, M.D., LL.D.," Volume V, 1907.

" Monograph "Diary of a Visit to the United States of America in 1883,"—Appendix by T. F. M., 1910.

" "New York's First Irish Immigrant Society," Volume VI, 1912.

" "Rt. Rev. R. L. Burtsell, D.D.," Volume VI, 1912.

" "Alexander J. Herbermann," Volume VI, 1912.

" "A Village Churchyard," Volume VII, 1914.

" "Rt. Rev. Patrick A. Ludden, D.D.," Volume VII, 1914.

" "Rev. Isidore Meister, LL.D.," Volume VII, 1914.

" "Rev. Malick A. Cunnion," Volume VII, 1914.

" "Rev. Michael J. Considine," Volume VII, 1914.

" "Rev. Joseph L. Hoey," Volume VII, 1914.

" "Adolph Francis Alphonsus Bandelier," Volume VII, 1914.

" "William Lummis," Volume VII, 1914.

" "Dr. James N. Butler," Volume VII, 1914.

" "James E. Dougherty," Volume VII, 1914.
" "Mission Work Among Catholics," Volume VIII, 1915.
" "Very Rev. Johann Stephen Raffeiner, V.G.," Volume IX, 1915.
" "John Doyle, Publisher," Volume X, 1917.
" "Sulpicians," (editorial comment) Volume X, 1917.
" "Diplomatic Intercourse with the Pope," Volume X, 1917.
" "Most Rev. John Lancaster Spalding," Volume X, 1917.
" "Right Rev. Henry Joseph Richter," Volume X, 1917.
" "Right Rev. Thomas A. O'Callaghan," Volume X, 1917.
" "Right Rev. John J. Kean," Volume X, 1917.
" "Rev. John T. Driscoll, S.T.L.," Volume X, 1917.
" "Rev. James T. Hughes," Volume X, 1917.
" "Rev. Remy Lafort, D.D.," Volume X, 1917.
" "Catholics in the War with Mexico," Volume XII, 1918.
" "Comments on the Baptism of Mother Seton," Volume XII, 1918.
" "Army Statistics in the Civil War," Volume XIII, 1919.
" "Comments on St. Louis Cathedral and Louis Le Couteulx," Volume XIII, 1919.
" "A Layman's Impression of Catholic Conditions in the Far East," Volume XIV, 1920.
" "Thomas Addis Emmet, M.D.," Volume XIV, 1920.
" "William R. King," Volume XIV, 1920.
" "Thomas S. O'Brien, Ph.D., LL.D.," Volume XIV, 1920.
" "The Hon. Eugene A. Philbin," Volume XIV, 1920.
" "Richard S. Treacy," Volume XIV, 1920.
" "Rev. Frederick M. Schneider," Volume XIV, 1920.
" "Michael J. Keilty," Volume XIV, 1920.
" "Edmund J. Curry," Volume XIV, 1920.
" "In Memoriam: President Stephen Farrelly," Volume XVI, 1924.
" "Lincoln's Opinion of Catholics," Volume XVI, 1924.
" "Some Records of the La Farge Family," Volume XVIII, 1928.
" "Tales of Old New York," Volume XVIII, 1928.
  a—First Catholic Office Holder
  b—Grand Opera's Pioneer Patron
  c—A Catholic Note on Poe's "Raven"
  d—A Famous Landmark Passes
  e—A Day in Greenwich Village
  f—The New York Emmets
  g—Number Twenty-four Vesey Street
" "The Oldest American Book," Volume XVIII, 1928.
" "Archbishop Hughes and Mexico," Volume XIX, 1929.

" "The Centenary of American Catholic Fiction," Volume XIX, 1929.

" "Two Pioneer Russian Missionaries," Volume XIX, 1929.

" "St. Peter's—Barclay Street," Volume XIX, 1929.

" "Catholic Traditions of the White House," Volume XIX, 1929.

" "Brooklyn's Proposed Cathedral," Volume XXI, 1932.

" "Giovanni Battista Sartori," Volume XXVI, 1936.

" "Catholic Action," Volume XXVIII, 1937.

" "Early Catholic Weeklies," Volume XXVIII, 1937.

" "Converts Who Became Bishops," Volume XXVIII, 1937.

" "Our Colored Catholics," Volume XXVIII, 1937.

" "Tales of Old New York," Volume XXIX, 1938.
  a—Mother Seton's Residences
  b—A Once Famous School

" "Catholic Lay Action," "General William T. Sherman and the Presidency," "New England Nuns," "Some Early Sodalists," Volume XXX, 1939.

" "The First Catholic Monthly Magazines," Volume XXXI, 1940.

" "A Dutch Irish Pact, 1860," Volume XXXI, 1940.

" "New York's Great Cathedral," "Early Days in Philadelphia," "North America's First Hospital," Volume XXXI, 1940.

" "Catholic War Chaplains," Volume XXXII, 1941.

" "The Ireland Family," "First Catholic University," "Catholic Historical Index," "The First American Novel," Volume XXXII, 1941.

INDEX

Adventures of Alonzo, 80
Albareda, A. M., 64
Allen, Fanny, 106
Alsop mansion, 83, 84
America, editorial on T. F. M., 47-48;
T. F. M. on editorial staff, 48, 81,
83, 91-93; first issue, 82-87; James
Gray, on staff of, 83; Rev. James J.
Daly, on staff of, 85; first staff, 86;
Rev. Thomas Campbell, on staff of,
86; Rev. Francis X. Talbot, on staff
of, 87-89; Rev. Paul Blakely, on
staff of, 89
American Catholic Historical Society,
T. F. M. on Executive board, 41;
T. F. M. made life member, 42
Anderson, Dr. Henry James, 96, 99
Andrews, William Eusebius, publishes
Truth Teller, 100-101
Astor, John Jacob, 98
Augustine, Sister Mary. *See* Barber,
Jerusha
Augustinians, early literary produc-
tions, in America, 74
Austin, Rev. John, 117
"Autobiography of T. F. M.", 29
Aztecs, 74

Backhous, William, 98
Baltimore Sun, T. F. M.'s daily letter
to, 24
Baptista, Sister Mary. *See* La Sal,
Charlotte
Barber, Abigail (Sister Francis
Xavier), birth, 108; enters Ursuline
Convent at Quebec, 114; death, 114
Barber, Rev. Daniel, 105-106; 110
Barber, Jerusha (Sister Mary Aug-
ustine), studies Catholic doctrine,
107; baptized, 108; first Commun-
ion, 108; enters Visitation Convent,
109; teaches, 110; visits with hus-
band, 113-114; death, 112
Barber, Josephine (Sister Josephine),
baptized, 108; enters Visitation
Convent, 115-116
Barber, Mary (Sister Mary Benedicta), birth, 108; writes about parents, 113; enters Ursuline Convent,
114
Barber, Samuel Joseph, birth, 108;
becomes Jesuit, 114; death, 114
Barber, Susan (Sister Mary Joseph),
birth, 108, 114; enters Ursuline
Convent at Three Rivers, 115;
death, 115

Barber, Virgil Horace, birth, 105;
minister, 105-106; visits Father
Fenwick, 107; converted, 107;
school at 24 Vesey Street, 108; be-
comes Jesuit, 107-108; at George-
town, 110; at Claremont, N. H.,
110; visits with family, 112, 113-
114; work with Indians, 113; died
at Georgetown, 113; 115-116
Barber family, other converts in, 110
Bay State Psalm Book, in Bodleian
Library, 77
Becar, Noel J., 98
Belford, Rev. John L., writes on T.
F. M., 36, 44
Benedicta, Sister Mary. *See* Barber,
Mary
Blakely, Rev. Paul L., eulogizes T.
F. M., 89-91
Bodleian Library, *Records and Stud-
ies* in, 77
Books, earliest printed in America,
73-74
Boston, 96
Boston Evening Gazette, 34
Brady, James, 105
Brady, Thomas, 105
Breslin, Rev. Joseph, 75
Brosnan, Rev. Jeremiah, 15
Brownson, Orestes, 19
Brooklyn, T. F. M. writes about, 35,
41, 63
Brooklyn Alumni Association, gives
medal, 50
Brooklyn Benevolent Society, organ-
ized, 98
Brooklyn Board of Education, Patrick
Meehan serves on, 12
Brooklyn Catholic Historical Society,
58
*Brooklyn Catholic Historical Society
Records*, Marc Vallette edits, 57n
Brooklyn Public Library, T. F. M.
trustee of, 35
Burtsell, Rev. R. L., 59
Butler, Mary Jane. *See* Meehan,
Mary Jane Butler

Cadley, Alfred B., 50-51, 56
Cadley, Katherine Meehan, 56
Cadley, Thomas Meehan, 56
Calvary Cemetery, T. F. M.'s interest
in, 31-32; 84
Campbell, Rev. Thomas, on *America*
staff, 86

Hayes, Patrick Cardinal, organizes "Catholic Writers' Guild", 23; letter to T. F. M., 34; letter to Notre Dame, 43; 75; 87

Hecker, Isaac, 19

Heeney, Cornelius, at Parmentier home, 36; gifts to St. Paul's Church, Brooklyn, 98; organizes Brooklyn Benevolent Society, 98; further charities, 99

Heffernan, John, editorial on T. F. M. in *Brooklyn Daily Eagle*, 33, 48-50

Herbermann, Charles, 59; president of U. S. C. H. S., 61; writes biography of Bishop Gabriels, 67

Herbermann, Elizabeth, visits Holy Father, 75

Herbermann, Louise, visits Holy Father, 75

Hibernian Chronicle. See The Shamrock

Hickey, Rev. David, 16; Prothonotary Apostolic, 46

Hispanic Society, presents *Doctrina Christiana* plates to Society, 72

Historical Records and Studies. See Catholic Historical Records and Studies

Hoey, Rev. Joseph, 15

Hughes, Rev. John, 40; T. F. M. meets, 63; closes Seminary at Troy, 68; *Life of John Hughes,* by Guilday, 70; buys Alsop villa, 84

Huneker, James, 21, 22

Huntington, Archer, 72

International Federation of Catholic Alumnae, T. F. M.'s interest in, 44

Ireland, Rev. John, in U. S. C. H. S., 59

Irish, in Civil War, desertion of, 65

Irish American, Patrick Lynch founder of, 11; Gaelic department established by Patrick Meehan, 13; T. F. M. joins staff of, 17; permanent files of, 40; *Truth Teller* merged with, 79; 100

Irish American Almanac, compiled by Patrick Meehan, 13

Irish Brigade, in Civil War, 63

Ironsides, Rev. George, 116

Italian Opera Company, first in New York, 96

Jesuits, early literary productions, in America, 74

Joseph, Sister Mary. *See* Barber, Susan

Josephine, Sister. *See* Barber, Josephine

Journalism, in colonial days, 78

Kearney, Rev. Raymond, 46

Kelly, Blanche Mary, on staff of *Catholic Encyclopedia,* 25; 44

Kelly, Leo, on staff of *Catholic Encyclopedia,* 26

Kenny, Rev. Michael, on staff of *America* 84

Kernan, William, 99

Kilmer, Kenton, 24

King, Percy, presents medal to T. F. M., 50-51

"Knighthood", 47

Knights of Saint Gregory, Joseph Bradley Murray, John Tracey made, 46

Kohlmann, Father, 114

Laetare medal, T. F. M. candidate for, 43-44; Shea, first recipient, 59

Lalor, Mother Teresa, superior of Visitation Convent, 109; aids Barber family, 112

Lambert, Rev. Louis, editor of *Freeman's Journal,* 20

La Sal, Charlotte (Sister Mary Baptista), 111

La Sal, John Baptist, 111

Lavelle, Rev. Michael, 94-95

Ledochowski, Rev. W., letter to T. F. M., 49

Lee, Charles Carroll, 59

Leopoldine Foundation in the United States, by Roemer, 71

Levins, Rev. Thomas, 104

Lloyd, Thomas, founder of American shorthand, 78

Log Cabin, Patrick O'Rourke, one of the publishers of, 18

London Truth Teller, 101

Long Island Catholic Historical Society, first meeting, 57; T. F. M., a trustee of, 57

Lynch, Dominic, 66; brings Italian Opera Company to New York, 96-97

Lynch, Patrick, founder of *Irish American,* 11, 79; last owner of *Truth Teller,* 83, 100; death of, 12

Lynchville, N. Y., 97